The Idiot

I Was a Lunatic from a Geordie Grangetown

I0118155

David Poulter

chipmunkapublishing
the mental health publisher

David Poulter

Published by
Chipmunkapublishing
PO Box 6872
Brentwood
Essex CM13 1ZT
United Kingdom

http://www.chipmunkapublishing.com

Copyright © David Poulter 2010

Chipmunkapublishing gratefully acknowledge the support of Arts Council England.

Foreword

Imagine a time when all relations amongst everyone and everything are honed down to zero. No good luck or bad luck, nothing saved or spent, all past interconnections exponentially dying out into a flat uniform state for all of creation. From then on good and bad fortune would be determined by individuals and their current intentions and actions for themselves, others and their environment.

Love or annihilation

David Poulter

Chapter 1

Hey have you heard...?

Hey have you heard of the Buddhist idea that we are ultimately alone? Perhaps 'we' is the wrong word – maybe it should be replaced by 'I' – but I think the concept is probably right. I blame consciousness. Yet lately I've been thinking that consciousness is like some sort of liquid we all have our heads stuck in. Therefore there are no individual thoughts, we all share the same thought patterns, so consciousness is like one big block of thought that we all use. Even animals. Obviously there are intellectual thoughts and emotional feelings, but who is to say these are not experienced by all living things? Clearly animals don't build nuclear reactors, but perhaps doggy emotions are the same as ours, so maybe our brains are just like receivers and only pick up pieces of consciousness they are designed to. Still what has this to do with feeling alone? From what I've just described I've even convinced myself that we are – nay the whole of creation is – involved with the same conscious bubble. Sounds cozy, so there is no need to feel alone. I bet now you expect me to come out with some long explanation to convince you that my theory of 'Creation' is right. Well unfortunately I'm clueless, I haven't any answers. I know jack shit. I've even convinced myself now that I'm not really alone. Perhaps doggy thoughts are even creeping into my head, maybe I'm that simple – my brain receives the same thoughts as dogs. There is some school of psychological thought that states that if you have a strong feeling, emotion or thought, you should analyze it, take time to meditate and find out the root of it.

A long time ago I felt complete. I was a child and everything was normal. Dad worked, mum stayed at home, I went to school. Yet as I got older I always used to look out of my bedroom window and think there have got to be better places in the world. Not that my parents were poor, on the contrary, we were middle-class. In fact I used to look back on my childhood and think I had some kind of 'Norman Rockwell painting' kind of existence, if that's possible. Maybe it's not, I'm from England anyway. Well understand this, reflecting on my youth with my family, the past seemed safe, snug and comfy. My perceptions have changed now; sometimes my childhood appears to have had more in common with 'Edvard Munch's The Scream'. Anyhow up until my middle thirties I thought of my parents as being pretty normal, even though there were a few blank spots in my mind. Still after I left home, I never really wanted to go back, not even to visit. It wasn't as though I hated them, the lethargy and apathy about going home had more to do with my laziness and I suppose selfishness.

As a young man I could be crude and cynical and usually had something better to do, some place better to go, even if it was sitting in my front room watching the television. I liked being away from them and somehow craved independence. The point is I didn't really love them, I think that's what I mean about blank spots. I never really considered it strange. I never considered it period. The person who really made me think about my family and my relationship with them was my wife. Hey I'm divorced now, true love didn't last. Nevertheless when we were together I had a lot of contact with my wife's family. Her mother was divorced and often used to visit us, also her brothers and cousins would usually fly over most years. On reflection they made the effort to see the children, they weren't coming over to see me. I was liked but I was just part of the furniture. Incidentally the kids weren't mine, my wife had had two former relationships that had resulted in children, both had been planned, but the fathers had faded away. The children had never met them and their fathers weren't in contact: I was a quasi dad. Anyway with all this coming and going of her relatives, my wife would analyze my family and my feelings for them and compare them with her own experiences. She would also talk about her mother, whom she would have long conversations with when she came over to visit. They would catch up on gossip, talk about the past, discuss world events and politics, talk of religion and art, the latest fads and fashions: the list was endless. All in German. Later after her mother had returned home she would relate it all to me in English, which set me thinking that I didn't have that sort of relationship or understanding with either of my parents.

There were levels of feeling and friendship that I never reached with my mother or father that my wife took for granted with her own mother. What was more surprising was I didn't care, I was pretty much indifferent. My wife thought it strange and would ask me all sorts of searching questions, probing deeper and deeper into my past to ascertain the reasons behind this bizarre situation. All the time I tended to answer vacantly. I never really avoided her questioning, but neither did I become overly protective nor emotional about my family. Gradually I started to formulate that my family weren't that nice. Not that they were downright evil, but all the original facts about them that used to occupy my mind had to be re-assessed in the light of my wife's illuminating opinions and experience with her own family. For a start my wife's mother was reasonably humble when compared to my parents. She was and still is I suppose always open to new viewpoints and perspectives.

None of her beliefs were cast in concrete, yet she was stable and possessed a strong personality. My family, I suppose I mean my parents, were smug, bigoted, self-made middle-class citizens. Rising through the ranks of the class system had given them a strong sense of identity and achievement, which I had always recognized, taken for granted, even approved of but never really analyzed. So where my wife's mother would sympathize and feel perhaps compassion for some sorry event in the news, my parents conversely would mock, ridicule and gloat. Their very success in life had made them into people with very little tolerance. A cliché no doubt, but what resulted from my upbringing and how it affected me later is not ordinary at all. I was part of this family, I was immersed in their influence, so what I experienced as a child I accepted as normal.

To some this may seem banal and boring. An everyday situation that is common in Britain: a middle-class man comprehending his life and disapproving of his conceited parents. How stereotypical. Well it wasn't really like that then, and it isn't really like that now. I never really consciously rebelled. Even as a student I was usually obedient and considerate. Left-wing politics and demonstrations bored the hell out of me, I was into my artwork, my first proper girlfriend and exercise at university, nothing else much touched me. My father kindly picked me up with my possessions at the end of every term and delivered me at the beginning. A very generous and caring thing to do, I did appreciate it at the time as well.

Yet along with this and definitely later, there was this overwhelming sense of self-importance that surrounded our whole family. At family gatherings – I have two sisters and a brother – there would be endless discussions about how their peers had failed miserably in lessons or at examinations. Or how my brother or sisters had triumphed in class, beating all competition to be groomed by the prof for better things. My father encouraged all this inquiring enthusiastically, beaming in delight at other people's failures and tutting at the reported so-called lackadaisical attitudes of our student contemporaries. Even as a twenty-one-year old I stomached all this, their collective auras encompassed me. During these discussions I wouldn't applaud or disapprove, sometimes the boasting and self-congratulation would embarrass me though. Generally I acquiesced and took part in the conversation on a minor level. It was only later in my life thirty-something and married, that I equated this behavior with the in-family bitching that continues to this day. That very attitude of judging friends, peers and colleagues, and mocking and ridiculing their gaffes infected the family. Broken up into smaller units my family bitched and back-stabbed and still does. So when my mother-in-law would visit and there might be some sad story of one of my wife's relatives having some difficulty in their life, there would be genuine concern, thoughtful advice given and sympathy. On the other hand, the same situation within my own family would result in betrayal, gossip, jeering and finger pointing with an "I told you so" attitude. So looking back I suppose my childhood was far from rosy, but then I've been bitchin' about them.

Today in my new life I try to have a balanced view, I try to be philosophical about everything, myself included. I would dislike to continually mock and criticize my family or myself, not only because I've been through something weird that's changed my outlook somewhat, I've also neglected them and they have changed themselves. There are stories, incidents, relationships and love I've never heard of, or experienced as I've been absent for long time. I reside in a foreign country on the other side of the world from the U.K. The lifestyle and the culture are totally different, the climate is hot and humid, I live below the Tropic of Cancer, indeed I could go and stand on it if I chose to do so. Still I have a longing to escape, just like I did when I left college all those years ago.

Chapter 2

Footsteps of the Anti-Christ

Have you ever been to Heddon-on-the-wall? It's a village in the county of Northumberland. Actually it's very near Hadrian's Wall hence the name. I'm sure you have heard of the wall built by the Romans. Currently the place may be more infamous for the initial outbreak of foot and mouth. I visited the place with my family once just after I'd left college. My mother always used to say I had a drop-out personality, even though I completed my degree course. Anyway the point is when I finished university I started wandering around Britain. My art course had come to an end and it was time to face the job market. I felt confused and depressed as I didn't really want to get a job. What could I do? My degree was in Fine Art. I had spent four years painting and drawing thoroughly involved in my favorite subject. Now it was time to get a job in an unrelated field and settle down to 'real life'. To quote my father on the matter: "It was high time I put my nose to the grindstone. 'The holiday' – i.e. my university course – was over and it was now appropriate to enter the 'real' world and to forget about swanning around." I balked at the idea. So I immediately contacted a college friend and made my way to Little Warley in Essex. I intended to find agricultural work. The summer stretched ahead and I didn't want to be confined to my hometown – a northern industrial mess situated on the east coast – or depressing job prospects.

I wanted to see beautiful views. I wanted the sun on my face. I wanted fresh air in my lungs. But I wanted something else. Something I just couldn't put my finger on. I planned to pursue it though.

While at college I had met Jan. She was from Essex and

during the summer months she and her brother often took up work on farms, partly for the money, partly to be out of doors, and ironically to relieve the boredom of long summer days. Apparently it was common, lots of people did it, and the work was often available. Being from an industrial town in the north this kind of lifestyle had never crossed my mind. So taking up an earlier invitation from her I left and caught the train to Upminster. My plan was to get a short-term job picking potatoes, save up as much money as possible, then travel. This sort of scheme would seem vague and foolhardy to most. I was lucky in having two things in my favor. Firstly, free accommodation kindly provided by Jan's parents. Secondly, a friendship and perhaps temporary travel companions in the shape of Jan and her brother Rob. The transition was smooth; I put my name down for agricultural work at the local employment office and got a job a week later.

The farm labor was both tiring, yet invigorating physically. Mentally it was utter tedium. The only thing that stimulated my mind was the occasional conversation. The scenery was a great inspiration though. I love landscape art, so naturally my eyes were drawn to its shapes, patterns and colors. The summer rolled on. I missed my graduation ceremony. It wasn't a form of rebellion, I was too content, too lazy to attend. Even though the work was boring, the outdoor lifestyle suited my temperament – I love pastoral environments to this day. Jan's parents were like friendly foster parents, or how I imagined them and she and her brother offered a double act of wit, humor and charm. My past became a blur, my future unknowable and inconsequential. Feelings for me are fleeting. I do relate to people at the time or in the moment, so I believe myself to be quite an emotional person when dealing with anyone. Then again the minute I'm alone my sentiments drain away and I'm left feeling completely blank. Even so I remember I enjoyed my time that summer. Apart from the farm work there were minor excursions, week-ends away and a few holidays. All this was possible because Jan, Rob and I pooled our resources and bought a cheap car. The first trip we took was to Devon, a long drive for sure. Anyhow for some reason the village of Highampton attracted our attention, I don't know why, maybe because it stands on a ridge and offers wonderful views of Dartmoor. I suggested driving down to Topsham for a look-see, but Jan refused. Rob and I were passengers, she was the only one with a driving license. I tried to tempt them with the idea that the Devil had purportedly passed through the place in 1855 and they both tittered. Eventually we returned home.

So my summer passed. I still see images in my mind years later. Pet rabbits hopping around the small semi's garden. Jan's dad laughing with a roll-up in his mouth. Electrical storms on humid nights. The sun rising as I cycled along the road to the farm. Jan and her mother preparing food in deep conversation. Rob watering his plants. They are like photographs in my mind. Sometimes big changes happen in our lives and we are unaware of their influences and causes. Various changes were happening to me. This was also true of my hosts. In the late summer Jan, Rob and I took a trip to Bromham, Wiltshire. Why I can't remember – the original idea was to head to Stone Henge – but somehow we didn't make it. I think Jan got sidetracked with the idea of buying soft fruit and followed homemade road signs. Anyway after this trip my 'foster parents' decided to make a big transformation in their lives.

They wanted to move house and change their lifestyle. Living in a cheap, boring, suburban environment bothered them. Doing menial and tedious jobs offended them. I could relate to them in a way, I understood their feelings of mediocrity. But one thing I could not do was encourage them to make the change and give them moral support. I could be of practical help though. They decided to move to an estate near Llancloudy in Herefordshire. I'm not talking about a housing estate, I mean landed property. The idea was to sell the small semi, bank the money, live in a tied cottage, and work for their "Lord and Master", as Jan's dad put it. A rural idyll I might have chanced myself had the opportunity arisen. Unfortunately the reality proved to be more of a rural tyranny. The estate a totalitarian one. Still to be selfish it gave me the chance to travel to new destinations; I used the area as a base for further excursions.

The farm work was over and I was traveling. My first trip was to Gaerwan, Gwynedd which is on the Island of Anglesey. This marked the beginning of a period of wandering alone, my friendships were still intact, but as individuals we chose different priorities. So as the days trickled by I crisscrossed the country, my camera in hand. I also made the occasional trip back to the North-East, to visit my family. These sojourns were always short and usually strained. I went back out of a sense of duty and necessity rather than any fondness. To be truthful though I think my family were patient with my lifestyle and attitude. Or did they simply not care? Whatever, at the time I considered none of this. It seemed I had an agenda stamped on my mind, it was though my wild itinerary was not even a choice. I was compelled by a blind instinct, like a bird migrating. Counties flashed by: Lancashire, Northamptonshire, and Devon again, Powys Wales, Herefordshire my 'home base', Leisterershire and Essex. By the end of summer I had banded up with Jan once more with the plan of heading towards Cumbria and thence onto Scotland.

On the journey we considered our finances, money or lack of it was becoming a priority and our first thoughts were to turn to the welfare system. We both chortled at the idea. At college grants from the government had sustained us. What could now? Jan had a few other notions of how to raise money and explained her various unusual ideas as she drove. Her words echoed and faded as I clandestinely dozed remembering the past. During our study at college part of the course had been a theoretical art history program. The actual syllabus was quite relaxed, but the amount of history we had to cover was laughable, due to the fact we started with cave art and moved progressively up to the present day. Any sane person could see the amount of effort needed was beyond the grasp of a workaholic genius if the subject was to be covered seriously and thoroughly. The fact is we couldn't and didn't. Saying that I still enjoyed the lectures, study and compositions, my favorite period was the European Renaissance. I often got romantic and idealistic about history generally and so did Jan. It wasn't so much the era, with its styles and fashions, but the mystery, particularly in connection with the landscape. I always imagined the earth as unspoilt and clean, a virginal place if you will.

Even today I envision there are places on this planet that are hidden, and perhaps remote, where no human foot has trodden. In the past, say five hundred years ago, the world was a different place physically, but also psychologically. The natural environment held sway over people's minds and perhaps common sense. A host of supernatural beings presided over the land and a lot of them apparently were best avoided. Superstition ruled. The landscape I traveled through with Jan was completely different: mapped from orbiting satellites, traversed by thousands of roads, crisscrossed with paths, pylons and telegraph poles strung with miles of wire. Fields, plowed, sown, sprayed and harvested in a never ending cycle. The very air zipping with micro-wave, infra-red and a whole collection of radio frequencies spawned by huge transmitter masts planted on prominent peaks. A constant stream of passenger planes cutting across the high atmosphere leaving a faint trail and noise behind them. And the occasional military jet screaming through the sky at low altitude. Our modern era. How did these things affect our lives? My drowsy reverie came to an end as Jan summed up her idea.

So what were her outlandish plans? Well long ago artisans, craftsmen and journeymen had wandered through the countryside from town to town offering their services. Read any biography of any famous artists from the Medieval times through the Middle Ages to the Renaissance and beyond, and you'll find a lot of them traveled for patronage and commissions. With this fact as a guide and an inspiration there must have been practically an army of minor individuals doing the same thing. We used this knowledge as a charm, a talisman to hold onto, something that might bring us good fortune and protection in our current age. Even so we were living in a fantasy land created by our own minds and I think we both secretly knew it. Others would judge us as playing at life. Indeed Jan made a joke that the only thing missing were our letters of introduction. References I thought, we don't have any references and current bank accounts.

We headed up to Carlisle and then onto Longtown on the river Esk near the Scottish border as we wanted to keep away from the hordes of tourists that frequented the Lake District. Arriving at noon we scoured the job center and local notice boards but found no work, nothing in the line we had to offer anyway. What did we really expect? Here was an agricultural town. A town with the largest sheep market in England. There were no market gardens, horticulture or potato farms, we knew that much before we arrived. What we had planned in our deluded minds was to offer our artistic services, after all we both had a degree in Fine Art. We might as well have had degrees in sculpting shit for all the demand there was. The car we had was a jalopy with a M.O.T. Test pending and we were living off our savings. Jan suggested we signed on the dole and I agreed. So we found the nearest caravan site and booked a static van for two weeks. It was officially autumn so the rates were reasonably low and the place was practically empty. All this had taken place in the summer of 1987 as I pursued my uncertain and obscure dream. I was following my feelings – perchance something was following me. It was unknowable and untouchable as my aspirations. Some years later a dark presence passed through the countryside trailing in my footsteps and blighting the landscape. Are things coincidental? Or do we carry curses?

Disasters, wars, pestilence and ill-luck. Beauty, harmony, abundance and good fortune.
Are they not just figments of manifest evil and good?

It felt like our world was coming to an end. Nothing worked. I have a feeling that registers when all is lost. It does not give me strength. All it does is warn me that either contingency plans have to be made, or any positive emotional expectation with reality must be totally abandoned. The pain is intense sometimes, but I know instinctively that all optimism needs to be given up. Clinging onto possible scenarios only offers hope. To really give the desired objective even the smallest of chances, one must absolutely relinquish all attachments to it, which is sometimes impossible. Desire unfortunately persists to minute degrees. Therefore I knew we were doomed. When I feel like this I hope the whole world might end.

I've read lots of stuff about the Armageddon and the Anti-Christ. Apparently the first one was Napoleon, the second Hitler and now the world is waiting for the third. Who will it be? And how the hell will we know before it's too late? For arguments sake the Anti-Christ doesn't appear in the Book of Revelation by Saint John. Check it out for yourself. Saint John only mentions the Anti-Christ or Anti-Christs in his first and second books. So watch out! According to him if you don't believe in Jesus as the Divine Son of God then you are *he*. Hey the Koran has loads of freaky stuff about the end of the world too – "When the goat herders build skyscrapers and men start to dress as women the end of the world is nigh." Lots of religions have end of the world scenarios. Then again how about Buddhism and reincarnation as well? How do they fit in? Hey I'm Spartacus...

Chapter 3

The way some people are

They are big boned and good looking, well fed and polite. They don't love you, but they don't hate you either, they seem indifferent. They are privileged and well groomed. They have a place in society and they are nice. Who the fuck are they? How do they fit into the great scheme of things? Here I am some skinny git worrying about my life. Hey! How can I enter your milieu? Perhaps I have to serve time and crawl up your arse. Bitterness. I hate life sometimes. Here we are stranded in a caravan in the North of England. We joked and amused ourselves about the future but ultimately our fears proved correct. No one is prepared to take us in or trust us. Jan and I are urban refugees, products of the late twentieth century, nothing but educated vagabonds.

To get a permanent address and welfare money you need the "Mark of the Beast" apparently: bank account details, credit rating approvals and professional references, these will secure you a home in this neck of the woods. Nowhere to rent, therefore no permanent address, hence no dole likewise. The weather hasn't helped either it has rained and poured. Our money, dreams and strength have drained away like the floodwaters. We have tried and tried, but every estate agency has said the same thing. No proper I.D. and references. No tenancy agreement. The welfare have hedged as they wanted a permanent residence and therefore were prepared to wait. We have failed as journeymen, I think life in the Middle Ages would have been easier. Retreat is our only option. Longtown near Carlisle has proved to be a disaster.

This is how it was. To some I'm a facetious, favored individual. A privileged young man with an arts college degree paid for by the government. Someone with a pampered, spoiled childhood and a middle-class status. Well, so what. I've always failed and felt a failure. Within every group, even my family, I have been the outsider kissing ass to be accepted. I seem to have spent all my life waiting. Waiting for the right connection, the right time and opportunity, the right person to arrive. I have set up various plans and carefully crafted schemes to ensnare good fortune, patiently standing by for months, fine tuning my strategies all for nothing. I must constantly fawn, grovel and boot lick. Toady, cringe and kowtow to gain the minutest successes.

So I had to connect with the ultimate 'beast' my father to achieve any forward path. I didn't want to go in this direction, however I felt I had no choice. I'm not religious, even so my pleas were answered. The secular world is hard to beat, it's a strong reality we can all relate to. I surrendered to it. The mind is willing, but the flesh is weak.

Months later I was settled in the Yorkshire Dales, living in rented accommodation in a small village. Valley after valley run off the central spine of the Pennines watershed, mostly to the east, the whole area is a National Park. Settlements date back to Viking times and beyond, perhaps even prehistoric trails meander through the hills. I immediately invited Jan to stay, but things were brittle between us as we had argued a lot when we had been marooned at the caravan site, torrential rain keeping us prisoners. So I gave up my persuasions and began my life as a hermit, collecting wood for the open fire, taking photographs and painting. I embarked on some government program, fantastically called "the back to work scheme" which I crudely named the back to bed scheme, although to be honest I did persevere with my art. Autumn had flared across the Dales inflaming my mind with desire; I so much wanted to capture its essence. I became obsessed with it: bark and leaves mulching wet and sweet with mushrooms, branches and twigs with tattered amber foliage, the golden orb of the sun low on the horizon giving rise to long indigo shadows and amongst all this, myself. I consumed it, I loved it, I wanted to become part of it.

My preoccupation with this was interrupted by two events: firstly a previously unknown neighbor called soliciting my labor, unfortunately as a stable yard worker and secondly Jan rang. That evening drinking beer I was secretly glad of both. For starters my so-called art business was really bombing and truth be told I was randy and lonely. While at college I'd been dating another girl, but we'd parted company and I'd befriended Jan. I considered this past of mine as I stared at the fruit bowl on the table: apples and peaches, their forms curving into miniature dark abysses. A private still life. My college relationship had promised everything, but had created no coming destiny. So I had ran and escaped, by throwing myself into a supposed true friendship with another – I thought I understood and related to Jan as much as my own self. The next day I rang back and repeated the invitation, then called to see my neighbor. Mrs. Grange opened the door on the first knock smiling profusely, completely attired in riding gear she took me to the stables adjoining the house where Phillipa and Teddy, Leopold and Ponette each greeted me. The first two were donkeys, the latter horses, all stabled and each standing on a mountain of shit. Curiosity and fear was what I saw in their eyes, I felt the same. Yet a desire to be close to them tipped the balance.

I accepted the job and Mrs. Grange led them out of the stables and into various fields. I was left slightly disappointed confronted by steaming piles of manure, still I've always had a compulsion for physical work. And hey animals have always enchanted me, even though my family never welcomed pets, the deprivation from my childhood only increased my attraction to them. I remember once as a teenager realizing the emotions they held: sentient beings without human intelligence, but with true feelings. I dug into the shit with renewed vigor; I knew with the right treatment they would love me.

Jan promised to appear the next day and made arrangements to do so, consequently I bought a second bicycle. Riding one and steering the other I made my way to the station. Risedale had no railway therefore I had to cross the Pennines to reach the Carlisle to Settle line. A beautiful sunny day with magnificent clear views, I reveled in it, I felt complete as my legs pumped the pedals up the gradients and freewheeled down the slopes. I was convinced I was meeting a confidant, my new counterpart in life who would perhaps one day know my mind.

She arrived banishing my loneliness and reflective solitude, bringing companionship and an eventual routine: boring yet comforting, a plateau of domesticity developed and a mutual ambition to be artists. We were becoming a couple with concerted efforts, however I still had that peculiar feeling plaguing my mind – the fruit on the table and my unsated desires. My college life had spawned an obsession: consideration of a curvaceous form, the flesh blushed pink with beads of moisture clinging to it, the cleft just visible realizing that familiar heart shape. Concentrating, I take one last look, my tongue sticking to the roof of my mouth, I swallow and grip the shaft harder. With my mind ablaze and my lips drooling I start rhythmically pounding, occasionally teasing the tip to resolve an agony in the creation. My rendering to beauty.

Originally Jan and I had just been friends. The summer jobs and traveling together had been a reciprocal exchange of give and take that suited our temperaments. The whole relationship had been so easy going, so without flaws it shocked us. Also there had been no real distance between us. The arguments had eventually arrived though, an inevitability caused by being cooped up together at the caravan site. I had blamed the bad weather but other truths were present. Some facts I hid and attempted to banish from my mind, nonetheless the tinny walls, the drumming of the rain and feelings of inadequacy created a vacuum that sucked past comforts and cravings into my mind. Ripe fruit.

Autumn transformed into winter and I shoveled wagon loads of dung. Mrs. Grange gave me other tasks to do: repairing dry stone walls, fencing and watering and grooming the horses. There is a certain feeling working with one's hands, especially in menial jobs. Being outdoors only enhances this perception. Then again maybe I have a special knack for work such as this. A joke? Maybe. I liked the chores and the environment. Working with horses also acted on my mind like a sedative. I became relaxed, the repetitive actions brought on a dream like state with 'horsy auras' wrapped protectively around me like blankets; their gentle minds pervading the air. Once they gained my trust they settled down and so did I. They loved me. With this meditative state came philosophical contemplation of life. I was aware tomes had been written on the subject of such things, nevertheless personal experience adds its own flavor. Mr. Grange was an ill man suffering from diabetes and a chronic form of arteriosclerosis, he had a prosthetic leg and poor sight. Conversely Mrs. Grange who was the same age was a retired doctor, the perfect wife and fit and healthy. Why do some people suffer so much? Why are some of us so cursed? An old chestnut for sure. Faith cannot be argued against, all the same some beliefs are more logical than others.

Right through the winter Jan and I pursued our artistic careers, traveled around the local area and socialized with the Granges, these convivial events always took the form of evening soirees. The fact that Mr. Grange was practically crippled obviously limited our activities and the venue, which therefore constantly took the form of food and drink and conversation at the Granges' home. Stories about the horses, laughter at the cats and dogs escapades and serious interchanges concerning the state of the nation were the standard topics of discussion. Chatting amiably into the night the initial feeling was one of camaraderie, an older couple entertaining a younger one. The gaiety was superficial however, happening to glance around the room one night as Mr. Grange hobbled across the floor pushing his wife away to assert some form of independence, I realized his bitterness, her despair and Jan's embarrassment, and also my detachment. These were the real predominant emotions which had been around all evening, hidden from view in the backs of our minds. The false atmosphere that had been pumped up like a bubble cushioning the conversation had burst. I made a polite excuse and left dragging Jan with me.

A spring day and I'm cycling up the lane to the Granges. The long fields that run up the fell are empty, the horses have either escaped or are still stabled. Clouds whisk over the crest of the escarpment, a lonely figure wanders below the ridge. I am perplexed. I reach the yard where a hose runs unattended, the dogs wandering about aimlessly jump up to greet me, but my attention is snatched away. A large unmarked car and the small local police van are parked by the house, I blink uncertainly as two tall men approach, they look stern yet act friendly. They ask a few questions as I'm led to the large barn, apparently I must feed the horses. I am told not to look at the small caravan parked within it, but the sacks of bran are close by. I sneak a furtive glance: Mr. Grange's prosthetic limb lies upon the roof, I'm nonplussed. I finish my task and turn to leave, catching site of the caravan window. The net curtains are dirty yellow with spots of brilliant crimson polka dotting them, I feel queasy. I pat the horses and go.

We have decided to leave the Dales. Mr. Grange is dead. His suicide has shattered his wife's mind. Jan does not feel comfortable. I am bewildered.

The Idiot

Karma: people either believe in it or they don't. It is the total effect of a person's intentions, actions and conduct during successive phases of a person's existence, regarded as determining the person's destiny. That is all very well but how does it operate? We react with our emotions, they color our lives. Happiness and sorrow, love and hate. These feelings are responses to situations. But then again people can become emotional due to various reasons, some things that affect one person may cause indifference in others. How can emotion be measured? Imagine a simple event in a sensitive person's life, like say dropping and breaking a favorite ornament. This accident may be emotionally equivalent of say falling out of a five storey building and breaking both legs for someone who is remote or thick-skinned. Physical matter as a tool of experience is a mysterious business. What is real?

Chapter 4

A brand new reality

Luminous turquoise breakers, bright foaming surf, a dark indigo horizon, flecks of white caps in the swell. Seagulls hang at various heights, floating on an offshore breeze, practically motionless and expressionless; they are like wooden toys or puppets. The small harbor with its fishing boats protects a dinky beach with the requisite golden sand and striped canvas folding deck chairs. White washed cottages ring the edge of the bay, with the occasional palm peaking out between.

We have made it with lots of planning, debates and deliberating. We have absconded taking all our belongings and leaving all our responsibilities behind, whether real or imagined they must be dismissed. Our destination is St Ives, Cornwall, but being from the North-East coast I find it hard to believe I am still in England, the color of the ocean and the radiant light are mesmerizing. I have never been this far down the peninsula before. My childhood memories are of Roker beach with its light brown sand, blue gray sea and small waves lapping at the shore, here people are surfing – riding emerald Atlantic rollers, the whole scene is surreal. Mr. Grange is forgotten.

England as a kingdom has so many diverse environments. Traveling a mere four hundred miles or so had changed our surroundings into an exotic subtropical paradise. Transfixed by all this beauty all thought of my past vanished. I was more concerned with the convenience of my contemporary world than the tragedy of Mr. Grange's death. Landscapes were so accessible now, I could change my reality by merely getting on a train and the proof of that fact was here. I was lapping up the sun when only a few hours ago I had been wrapped up against the cold in a false spring in the Dales. Living in the Middle Ages as a journeyman must have been hell, to be bound by horse or foot, superstition and convention. I felt *free* again with my government scheme and this new inspiring landscape. Maybe success was possible after all. Since I was practically independent of my family emotionally and financially my confidence and self-esteem blossomed. Behold for the first time in my life I truly felt I ruled my destiny.

Yet destiny had amusing tricks to play in the form of Jan's waywardness, something I had never considered. Perhaps fate's clock had been ticking away and my preoccupation with my 'fruit' and an abandoned college relationship needed recompense. Or were these ideas, just figments of my imagination, a useful fabrication that convinced me that I understood life and was therefore above others. Yet another theory to cling to for protection. I'd never given a thought to the fact that Jan had simply fled in shock from an uncaring partner and a lonely lifestyle, which had been turned upside down by a close neighbor's self-destruction.

We paid the deposit on the flat, ironically opposite the unemployment office our sponsors, and I immediately set to work painting furiously, determined to capture the feeling to life I craved. Jan went out to investigate the town and what she found changed our lives: paratrooper boots, ex-army fatigues, pierced noses and dreadlocks. A displaced band of individuals inhabited the area, living off the dole in cheap winter lets, council houses and even sleeping rough. She came home shopping one day full of excitement about the new friends she had met. How open and amiable they were. How full of interest. "A new face in town, an artist? Did she want to go to a party? Did she want some hash? Could she lend some money?" Conversely she was fascinated with the hairstyles, the tattoos and the gossip. Her attraction to the scene only compounded my horror. Jan was enthralled by her find. I according to the lingo was 'freaked'.

I decided to ignore her interest in her new found friends, choosing to study the light and take photographs. I perused local galleries and beach combed looking for interesting objects for my still life compositions: driftwood, pebbles and shells. Jan gradually disappeared from my life, meeting me occasionally at daybreak or bedtime, until one day I came home in the early evening and found to my surprise that the door to the flat was stuck.

I had managed to enter the communal hallway, but the door to my apartment was seemingly jammed. It felt as though a large bag of potatoes was in the way. I kept pushing as the object seemed solid yet somehow yielding. I eventually entered the living room only to be confronted by a large crowd of people all sitting on the floor. Indeed the obstruction blocking the door was a bearded individual who smiled and nodded as though I had arrived late. Jan was in the midst of them all chatting amiably. A haze of fragrant blue smoke hung in the air, electronic music played from our cheap cassette player. No one seemed to care as I stood there in the corner of the doorway feeling alienated and indignant. At college I'd always felt in charge of my life, as my fellow students followed certain rules. I could see in their faces they were controlled by obligation and discipline. My reality here was a different one. One glance and I knew I was out of my depth, here their expressions and the look in their eyes challenged my parameters in life. What I allowed and considered taboo were inconsequential in this scene.

I was scared as much as Jan was in her element. This personal space of mine and Jan's as well I suppose, had been invaded and nothing appeared to be sacred. Picking my way through the crowd I headed for the kitchen picking up snatches of conversation about "E's" and someone joining "the convoy", whatever that meant. The flat actually had a kitchenette and it took me several minutes to get there, the smell of frying reaching my nose long before I arrived. As I guessed it was standing room only, every surface and seat were taken, someone even occupied the sink. Jan and sometimes myself accompanying her usually shopped once a week storing our goodies in the small cupboards provided – well all the food and groceries seemed to have been found and were being passed around, everyone was munching away with a contented air. I was even offered a remaining biscuit. Packages and wrapping along with discarded half eaten munchies were dropped to the floor, trodden underfoot and mixed with cigarette ash and butts. The general chat was that politics was a crock of shit. Stifling a scream I retreated, gently pushing my way through boogieing bodies, the trance music suggesting I remain cool and 'groove', approaching Jan I let my anger rip.

I feel at sea so to speak. Lost. Jan has disappeared from my life. The flat is quiet as I practice my art. I chat in my mind to her, working all the while, I quietly explain that I must be in charge; I have no time for delinquents. Suddenly there is a knock on my door and I freeze, opening it I find Jan standing outside and immediately I feel insecure. I'm ready to negotiate and make concessions. Her conversation is genial but distant, she explains that she is living at a friend's house, some woman. She has a favor to ask though, hesitating she stares at the floor. I inquire. Her brother wants to stay for a while, there has been some trouble and he needs a place to crash. I acquiesce. She nods her thanks and turns to leave as I try to explain my thoughts and feelings, but I can see a remoteness, almost a coldness in her eyes. I guess my insistence in abandoning Mrs. Grange infects her mind still. I let her go.

Rob arrived a few days later, his familiarity bringing me comfort. He had been to a college in Wales but had dropped out, his explanations about his departure from studying nothing more than hot air, secretly I disapproved, but out of loyalty and friendship I let him stay. I had originally shared his bedroom at his parents' house while working on the farms. Two things strike me now as obvious: he let me into his life and private space without complaint or criticism and I'm more like my father than I think.

Looking back Rob and I got on well initially, we seemed to have the same opinions regarding life, eschewing crowds, trends and casual company, preferring the intimacy of a closer friendship. But then again aren't fears, dislikes and hatred a binding force in our lives? We drank beer and smoked into the night chatting about various topics, our young serious minds earnestly engrossed in intellectual theories, concepts and witty insights that had absolutely no bearing on our cheap and now squalid reality. With Jan remaining on the periphery, almost dropping out of our lives the flat became a shit-hole, often is the case with idealists, they are rarely practical people. We lived an inner glory, basking in our speeches, philosophies and visions, envisaging that bright future that awaited when the opportunity arose to reveal our genius. At present, fact was we eked out our meager existence from government welfare handouts, taking advantage of special schemes and projects designed to help the unemployed. We really had no intention of finding or even looking for regular employment, playing an outward appearance of sincere job hunters, we secretly mocked the system, imagining the day when we might be discovered, and fame and wealth would be forced upon us.

Jan meanwhile lived out her existence in the local woods dwelling in a 'bender' – a yurt like tent made from cut saplings and canvas – chanting mantras and fucking, or so my bitter mind suggested. Whatever. She had joined some modern day bohemian traveler type group, their 'uniform' ironically being from ex-army store stock, heads shaved at the sides, dreadlocks running down the back. She would occasionally appear at the flat accompanied by a new friend and a camp dog with a view to 'borrowing' some item that we would never see again.

Over the weeks Rob and I built up a pattern, a routine so to speak and being night owls and now binge drinkers we rarely got up until the afternoon, unless the dole office demanded some interview. Later we would skulk about the town and local beaches, sometimes meeting familiar faces from Jan's woodland encampment or even Jan herself, yet Rob was my constant companion, my alter-ego. He monopolized my life, a refreshing change from past girlfriends. For some reason I've always found most men dominating, even considered them dangerous, but he had a gentle nature and humorous take on things. And even though he was somewhat younger than me I sensed I was being looked after, protected, as I imagined an older brother might. A mentor-protégé relationship developed. So when the autumn once again rolled around and the tourists and the fine weather eventually deserted the town, and Rob suggested we leave and start a new and better life in Wales with his college friends, I readily agreed. He wanted to realize his aspirations, his dream was to squat some residence, write and influence society, alter public opinion and generally live out his ideals. I admired his resolution and wanted to do the same. We informed his sister and left. Later I rang my family.

"Hey have you ever considered what reality really is? In other words the bottle I'm drinking from, the alcohol in it, the stink from my feet. Me and you included. Everything. Apparently according to scientists it is all to do with atoms. But what the fuck is an atom? Ask any of them or look it up on the net and you'll find various theories. What is accepted by the scientific community though is quantum mechanics. I think it is still agreed it is the observer who determines the result. God the dog loves to lick my sweaty feet. Another idea is called 'super string' theory. Basically all reality is a vibration from another dimension. Imagine some cunt is playing music and we are the result. Let's hope the bastard doesn't hit a bum note.

Scientists say atoms are perhaps as old as the universe. Therefore so are we. Whatever. What I want to know is who else or what else has been using them? Fuck!"

Chapter 5

Wales, migrating

This is the story of my life. Yet there are others who will accuse me of being false, I hope they do not, for they do not know me for who I actually am. That I will leave this place like my other homes I am certain. It is just another stepping stone on my journey somewhere. I crave peace and tranquility, and although I have feelings about this place and time that I would really like to verify, I feel uneasy and want to slip away. Wales is certainly beautiful, but unsafe. Rob has joined a group of political activists, peers and old friends from college. I don't like their attitudes or their ways, so now I live alone, thank God. I found accommodation and work, a story in itself, suffice to say the derelict chalet that was originally a squat was bought out from underneath the squatters. Rob and the 'anarchists' moving on to live up to their political beliefs. I remained and the landlord now employs me to do occasional building jobs. But still I'm having problems: financial and otherwise. Fuck it! What am I going to do? Furthermore I keep having a recurring dream which bothers me. A playback or a repeat condition from childhood? Whatever. I appear to be studying something. A book? I'm not sure. A picture perhaps, I'm really engrossed in it anyway. It's like a puzzle, only it seems significant. Suddenly I realize the meaning and I'm scared. Why? Is this important to my life? It bugs me.

The sun is setting over the sea as I walk back to my home along the coastal footpath. I am content I suppose with the routines and labor such as I have found here. I have worked all day alone digging a cesspit. The ground has an attraction though, the color and the strata of the rocks continued to draw my attention as usual, they are part of a secret landscape beneath our feet. I love the dirt beneath my fingernails, the dusty feeling of my clothes, ironically I feel wonderfully clean. I'm unsullied of conversation or gossip. My thoughts have been pure and beautiful like the surroundings I have worked in. Now and again I have taken a rest and looked towards the horizon of blue meeting blue, the sea and the sky: a paradox that gives me the desire to paint once more. Everything can seem perfect in such an environment. Yet problems bug me like fireflies as sunset approaches, and with the day's activities coming to an end my thoughts are free to fly without constraint, and even though I swat them away my fears constantly return to crawl across my mind. I've lost touch with Jan completely yet I feel no real loss now, it's my nagging desires, sex and companionship that plaque my spirit.

Their lack in my life being constant foes. Rob has disappeared with a band of people I can barely describe never mind understand: 'hard-core anarchist vegan activists' is as about as close as I can define them. I sometimes miss his company, but he is determined to be part of their group and is completely committed to their cause. They want to "smash the system" and take over, they really do plan illegal covert activities, whether they carry them out I don't know, I didn't want to get involved, their zealot like nature scared me. Perhaps there is some connection with my dream, maybe the book or picture I'm studying is an analogy of my life, a riddle I solve yet the answer frightens me.

In the past I had always made friends with women more easily than men, frequently I found men threatening for some reason. To be sure I was always completely attracted and still am to women sexually, therefore I always considered myself normal. I'm not deviant, perhaps that is the wrong word, I don't want to appear prejudiced. Anyway the women I made friends with and the women I desired never coincided for whatever reasons. Passion was always lacking. Or is that sex drive? Libido? Is this a truth or just some puny stereotypical situation? Sometimes I guess it may just be the latter and my misjudgment.

My landlord is okay, he is somewhat older than myself but appears to have a normal life and doesn't look for challenges beyond his capability or reason, and as far as I judge him he seems safe. I certainly hope he is. In the past I usually felt marooned in a group of my peers. Rob's bizarre band of 'idealists' certainly proved the point. The aggression, domination and subservience always seemed to give rise to nothing but madness, being alone would appear more preferable. Yet I do want a companion I can relate to and I must fuck as well, the feeling is imperative. It is my insanity I think. Give me sex and friendship combined with a rural idyll and I'm sure I'd be content. Is this idiocy for my age? I have no one to ask advice from. I'm not in touch with anyone, even my family.

I met a local woman, or so I thought, at a local store. She smiled at me, two young children in tow. I smiled back then glanced at her figure as she paid the bill. I felt crass doing this. Living alone makes me forlorn yet aloof, so I constantly judge others and myself. Ultimately I'm the same as any man I think. Even so I dislike such lecherous feelings. Much later I found out she was German. Why am I so attracted to her? One reason is obvious she's beautiful, but there are other factors affecting the situation, that is obvious as well. I feel she is safe for some reason. Generally I judge most men the opposite. When in their presence I usually experience discomfort, old or young no matter they eventually disturb my mind. In their company I find I must follow or lead, this may be true with any friendship with either gender, yet within a male milieu I always witness such extremes in temperament and action and often stupidity. Am I abnormal? This question remains unanswered, as with any personal experience it is impossible to ascertain the truth. Admittedly I am insecure, any group of men induces this feeling within me and lately I have continued to avoid such circumstances rather than be involved. I basically flee or sometimes remain on the fringes until I have acquired what I need or want. This is not usual I realize but what is? I don't want to become fully involved, neither do I want to continually analyze my emotions as it makes me angry. For God's sake I know what I want from life, so I constantly steer myself in that direction. Men gathered in a group usually function as a whole, but rarely have I found myself comfortable as an integral part in these situations.

I understand that this is a difficulty, yet it is something I avoid easily. As long as I gain my requirements, I feel no loss, I can manage without sincere contact or so I imagine. Besides I don't like crowds anyway, never mind a bunch of men. As a child I liked playing with other children, I don't think gender was an issue. At home I usually hung around my elder sister. I sometimes remember being terrified of my father. Puberty brought a change of school, 'an all boys', believe me I suffered, I hated it and all the extra study. My fellow students in my view were no more than day to day classmates and therefore long term potential foes, no one was to be trusted. I was superficially friendly with everyone, but never really felt comfortable, I just wanted to get through the day as quickly as possible and get back home. I shied away from violence, aggression and sport. However I am observant, so please believe me when I say I did recognize true friendship, admiration, and maybe even love between my peers. I left the place at sixteen and never looked back, glad to be shot of the lot. Have I missed out on life? Possibly. Why was I like this? I don't know but I found out eventually.

My landlord is my only acquaintance and we have minimum contact, a distant father figure who makes requests which I obey always without question. This is subservient and archetypal behavior on my part, but I accept it as I know I must survive. I'm not even cynical about this as I realize the art world and life are far more complicated than I imagined.

The Idiot

Maybe I'm unlucky or maybe I'm not talented enough. Even so this question could be irrelevant, also I have no real way of answering it anyway. The real facts are my government scheme is coming to an end, life is fickle and I must persevere. As I dig the cesspit I ruminate on life, but please understand though I'm not complaining or bemoaning my fate. My fears usually arrive at nightfall. With hard labor abstractions and theories sometimes enter my mind, and these thoughts often come unbidden, as unrelated ordinary objects and situations in my everyday work seem to trigger their conception.

I recalled my art history course from college the other day: I was cutting rock with a pick axe when the colors and the patterns on the stones attracted my attention and reminded me of something. The whole area is sedimentary rock, layered like a cake, the strata were pushed up above the sea millions of years ago. Consequently it breaks away in sheets and has various degrees of hardness and thickness, occasionally I reach a layer of soft clay and the chiseled edge of the pick disappears into it, effortlessly, only to clang against the new rock layer below. Pinks, purples, mauves, crimson, blots, swirls, lines, geometric shapes, pattern the fragments I pull from the ground. Ridiculously one large thin sheet reminded me of a fauvist painting, some effort by Georges Braque, I can't remember the title, a still life anyway. Which got me thinking what lucky individuals some of those artists were. Hey I'm sure you've heard of Picasso, along with Braque he sold Cubism to the world, after his exhibition in Paris he was an overnight success.

I once read an anecdote about his life, apparently while painting in the south of France, a business man noticed him. The guy was immediately attracted to Picasso's painting and at once offered him a villa in exchange for it, which Picasso readily accepted. Imagine the power, the glory of such a thing, an afternoon's work translated into such a luxury. I on the other hand seem to have more in common with Vincent Van Gogh. I'm sure you know his life story and the tragedy involved: not a single offer for his work, perhaps he sold one painting, I'm not sure, he was supported by his brother I think, lived in poverty and committed suicide. Hey life's strange, both were talented and original artists yet fortune arrived too late for one. Why do these things happen? Life is unfair, the art world is capricious, so I dig cesspits and house foundations to support myself, occasionally I sell a painting, but I cannot survive on the income. I have set my sights on Ireland – "the land of poets and priests", if that's the right quote, I cannot remember. I know the population is very low, a great place for solitude no doubt. The German woman came to visit yesterday, perhaps that's a misstatement. She happened to be walking along the coastal path and saw me digging on a building plot nearby, so invited herself in through the gate and started a conversation.

Since our encounter I have started seeing her regularly, apparently she is living on welfare, a feat she managed somehow, I didn't dare ask too many details. Maybe if one is persistent enough the social welfare office pay out, like Jan and her band of woodland dwellers, stinking and filthy and living rough yet supported as unemployed and considered available for work. Conversely my German friend Hilda looks like a model, her two children angels. Both fathers are absent, English and apparently never in touch, perhaps that's why she receives single parent's allowance. I act at all times politely in her presence, yet my mind is a 'cesspit' of lust as her face and figure have that classical appeal my first girlfriend at art college had. But this time I'm sure the time is ripe.

Her children are amusing, for some strange reason they seem familiar to me, possibly they remind me of my elder sister and myself. They have my trust now and both crave my attention which is understandable I suppose given their lack of a father. My sister usually protected me, or so I have always imagined, sometimes she would just stand by and blankly watch as punishments were doled out, obviously some things were beyond her control. Neither disgust nor approval passed through her mind I think, just a general fascination for situations she had tried to prevent, but could do nothing about. I saw this same attitude in the eldest, a protective manner yet a certain resignation for circumstances beyond her jurisdiction and an interest in the later events. Hey not that I was punishing anyone, ironically I was as bad as the daughter I analyzed. I was really 'child' number three. Generally it was Hilda's youngest one that got into trouble, not because of any stereotypical young male mindset I might add, he just was excitable and forgetful, something his mother punished him for. We, the daughter and I, stood on the sidelines and watched.

I do not judge Hilda as a mother, it is something beyond my experience. That she has frustrations and anger with her life is normal. She also has an insightful and eloquent side to her personality and is not afraid to pry into my life and mind. Yesterday we were discussing dreams and I mentioned my own recurring one that has faded recently. She stated that sometimes we fear our own greatness, our own triumph, and dreams that can be both literal and metaphorical give us clues to the right direction. Hilda thinks the dream is about my own success, she also believes in me and my artistic abilities, so I have taken her interpretation of my dream as an inspiration. I have sworn to study art and famous artists again to look for ideas to motivate myself. I will begin with Durer, a German artist from the fifteenth and early sixteenth centuries, he is a favorite of mine. Once again I feel attached to an ideal and am optimistic. With the right attitude and guidance I will eventually sell my work apparently. My nightmare is now forgotten as I forge my new course.

Hilda and I are now lovers, constantly chatting and fucking, our joint dream is to move to Ireland, so I have started doing as many extra building jobs as I can as we have to save. Apparently since the Republic is so under populated there are cheap cottages with land to rent. We'll most likely leave in the early autumn, I've bought a transit van and we might be able to get hold of an old caravan. The children are excited and dance gaily around me as I mix concrete. The youngest Ivan is very affectionate, every time I stop to take a rest and sit down he puts his arms around my neck. He is only three and cannot say much, perhaps because his mother speaks both German and English to him. The eldest Sasha is seven, but she has air of sophistication about her and wit, her initial shyness and self-consciousness have evaporated and she now calls me "Pretend Dad" and giggles. I like their presence, they are innocent and beyond judgment, their affection and love have wrapped around me and I am insulated from the harsh loneliness of before. The summer now passes by with alacrity, time is moving with a greater tempo, as there is meaning in my life again and a destination to prepare for. Hilda has been to Ireland before so she relates anecdotes and experiences while fussing over the children, who stare in delight, yet mute silence at our exchanges. I feel as though my very thoughts have been hi-jacked, I cannot comprehend how new feelings, impressions and influences have invaded my psyche. My past self seems to have vanished in the presence of this instant family.

It's dusk and we are leaving tomorrow. Wales is certainly lovely in parts but gossip and the close proximity to New Quay and tourism and all that goes with it mars our lives. We both want a new start and seclusion. The sun has just set and I'm outside on the porch smelling wood smoke and listening to the distant sound of the waves. The far off 'V' of the valley frames the sea. The sky over head is banded in ever deepening shades. I love all this, such surroundings fill me with warmth. A steady tearing of grass interrupts my pleasure, a feeling of heaviness and power prods my mind. It's the night's scent that tells me of the intruders in the area. The wild ponies have

The Idiot

broken into my garden, no loss as there is only grass there. The children come onto the balcony their eyes wild with fascination. Foals and mares chew contentedly. Do I really want to chance my luck and leave this place? Does destiny exist? Or is life mere chance, a random event? I prefer to believe in fate, something that molds our lives. Still I have my reservations about going, but we have chatted so much and agreed. We both have this dream of freedom, to escape the constraints of this area and hopefully find something better.

Chapter 6

Melencholia

Hey I was looking at Albrecht Durer's Melencholia the other day, I've actually seen it many times before, not the original but copies in books. I assume you know the picture or I should say engraving I'm talking about. Completed in fifteen-fourteen it shows an angel sitting in a melancholic state staring into space, scattered around this figure are various anomalous objects. On the top left side of the print is a distant view of the sea with a rainbow and a comet.

A town is on the shore, with a wave threatening to inundate it. On the right there is part of a building close up and mysterious magic square, below this the angel sits contemplating. Life? God? Melancholy? Most interpretations say the angel is a she and is in a melancholic state due to lack of inspiration. As soon as I saw the picture I thought 'she' was a man, the hands are massive. 'She' could lay bricks I thought with those hands, also his shoulders indeed his whole figure suggest a male body. Some say Jesus. To me he looks like some young Viking warrior. Sitting next to him on a millstone, a feature I failed to mention earlier is a small child or cherub, inscribing on a plate or block. He reminds me of infants from Madonna and Child paintings popular throughout the Renaissance, indeed the oblique circle of the foreshortened scales pan – one of the objects around the figures – that hangs above his head is reminiscent of a halo. Ha ha, I'm beginning to sound like one of those boring art historians. Hey those Renaissance Madonnas were really feminine, even sexy, not like this bull-working hermaphrodite angel in Durer's engraving.

Not that I'm suggesting the figure here is a mistake or crudely drawn, for one thing Albrecht could draw and paint exceedingly well. Have you ever seen his piece of turf or hare? Complete realistic compositions from the early sixteenth century, the guy was a genius in a way. An artist painting pieces of ground when everybody else seemed to be painting just religious iconography. He was definitely into God. So he intended the angel to look a certain way. Perhaps if we develop perfectly in this human realm we exhibit certain features that are both male and female. But even that considered when I look at Melencholia and the seated figure I think of the angel as a young man without hesitation. When I first saw the engraving I was fascinated, there is so much detail and the whole feeling of the composition is one of mystery. The objects around the two figures seem to have no connection.

The consensus opinion is they are symbolic of something. The question is of what? On the ground in front of the contemplating angel from right to left are the following: a nozzle from a bellows, some nails, a ruler, a saw, a woodworking plane, a depth gauge, and a perfect sphere. A pair of pliers or grips protrudes from under his clothing near his feet. Traveling up the left-hand side of the picture are a lamp, a sleeping dog, a hammer, a polyhedron, and a crucible. These objects connect with the base of a ladder which leans against the building I mentioned earlier. Fastened to this structure, running across the top of the picture are a pair of scales, an hour glass and a bell which has the magic square underneath. A rope attached to the bell trails off the picture to the right.

To be honest, the initial feeling that struck me was one of uncertainty. It seemed to me the angel had some unfinished task to complete. His posture and face evoke a mood of deep thought, some problem to solve. A collection of keys are fastened to his belt and a purse is at his feet. He fiddles with a pair of calipers that act like clock hands as they are in the center of the picture, the objects arrayed around like numbers. The rainbow and the comet in the background symbolically suggest both hope and doom. Even the small coastal town is threatened by a wave. However any viewer is drawn to the magic square in the top right-hand corner. The engraving is notorious for this. It's a four by four square and each of the rows and diagonals add up to thirty-four. All of the numbers are drawn correctly apart from the five and the nine. These digits are both next to each other in the left-hand vertical column, the five above the nine with sixteen and four above and below them respectively.

The strange thing is the five is inverted and printed over what looks like a zero – perhaps a six – and the nine is a mirror image. Also on closer inspection the nine is composed of a zero and what looks like a small fish, its head hooked over the bottom of the zero. To my eyes the fish even looks like a miniature two. Now all this may seem very complicated, but read upwards the two digits could be seen as a date, two thousand and five for example. For some reason I found this very disturbing. The only other thing that caught my attention was the symbolism of the ladder and the other objects on the building. The picture seemed to be saying: climb the ladder to heaven where there is justice, represented by the scales, and time, represented by the hourglass will sound the alarm, represented by the bell. But who is ringing the bell? The rope disappears off the picture. That nagging thought dogged my mind. Who is sounding the alarm? The rainbow and the comet. Good fortune or disaster. The little peaceful town the wave has yet to reach.

Over the months I got totally absorbed. Obsessed really, the engraving took over my mind. I was convinced it was a message of some kind. An admonition. I thought some secret code must be embedded in the picture somewhere. Obviously in the magic square and the objects scattered around the two figures. The calipers at the center acting like the hands of a clock. So I set to work. The months past. It became my secret hobby, a priority almost. One afternoon a statement popped out of my deliberations. Everything fitted together logically and concisely. There was no error. There was no jubilation on my part either. The words scared the hell out of me.

Looking back now I know I chose logic and contemplation to relieve myself of any panic. It was only a picture in a book. The script or statement I had seemingly revealed was really only a product of my crazed mind. I have often thought that realities are just our personal experiences. We construct huge mind scapes and sometimes they are utter rubbish, therefore our minds are cluttered with emotions and thoughts that have no real bearing on our lives. Oh to get rid of such bunkum to make room for fresh ideas, feelings and inspiration.

I also contemplated on the life of Albrecht Durer; I had researched and read so much. The guy was super talented, there was no denying that. I saw him as the great master of Europe, painting one of the first true self-portraits and recognizable landscapes, a man of science who also created printed maps on spheres and celestial star charts. So imagine living in fifteenth and sixteenth century Germany. We look back on history and sometimes think it as romantic. The reality must have been complete squalor and ignorance for the most part. The amount of superstition at the time must have been immense. So really his achievements were truly amazing, and here I was thinking I had cracked some secret occult message left by a genius which had eluded experts over the centuries. I tittered to myself. A brief recollection of a past dream never touching my mind.

Chapter 7

Carraigulla

I spent thirteen years living in a cottage in Ireland. I moved there when I was twenty-six and left when I was thirty-nine. I arrived in company, I left single, a large part of my life which is strange and sad. I had met my wife in Wales, she had two children from previous relationships and was slightly older than me. I was young, stupid, idealistic, and conceited. She was sexy, cosmopolitan, unconventional and foreign. We both had the same dream of running off to Ireland and escaping the modern world, you see at the time the Republic of Ireland was a relatively poor country compared to the rest of Europe.

The plan was this: pool our savings, acquire a van and catch the ferry to Cork. Buy a map when we arrived. Any member of my family would freak at such plans, organizing a day trip for them would probably occupy twice as much time. Consequently looking back now I would consider myself and my wife as courageous but foolish. I saw a shooting star the night before we left and made a sincere wish, today I would consider such superstitions as prayers and regard them as important. Anyway the invocation may have worked as the trip was uneventful and the weather beautiful for autumn. I left the port of Ringaskiddy and Cork city immediately after disembarking from the ferry and headed towards the west, van and caravan, all my worldly possessions and my quasi instant family. I felt great, I felt I belonged, ironically I felt free.

Ireland was like a time-trap, I sensed I had stepped into the past. We spent one month driving and parking up anywhere permissible, asking questions in local shops, drinking in pubs and following any possible lead or invite. The people, the customs and the rural life shocked me. I wanted to mock it and scream in their faces that it was the 'late twentieth century'. Contrarily I was also drawn to it all, fascinated by the traditions, superstitions and the quaintness. The love and protection village communities had for their own inhabitants was beyond my belief, the feeling of unity was overbearing to the point of claustrophobia. Yet I know now this was perhaps my warped sense of judgment and even though their love for each other seemed to border on the unconditional I realized as I do now that I was an outsider, I was not some invisible observer beyond time and space. What occurred outside my presence was unknowable.

We drove to West Cork and onto the Beara Peninsula. The west coast of Ireland is shredded where fragmented rock and fingers of land embrace the sea. The Atlantic Ocean stretches to the shores of the American Continent. Marveling at the idea that I was on the edge of something with nowhere else to go unless I built a boat I felt I had found a home.

We camped in forestry entrances and on scraps of land, any local police or village people considered us as itinerants. Most were polite even if distant, a few curious and amiable. We told them we were looking for a house to rent. Let me explain, any normal couple would have chosen the accepted usual procedure of moving. We didn't, as my wife's and my own belief systems matched, that is to say we had a cosmic attitude and strongly believed in destiny. This conviction has run throughout my whole life. Take your pick: laziness, acceptance, stupidity, simplicity, arrogance, innocence, shortsightedness, faith, the philosophy has worked and failed from leaving home to this day. Others may always plan meticulously every detail: back-ups, insurance, contingency plans, everything worked out to the nth degree, then their plane crashes. The universe appears to guarantee nothing. Thank God we were lucky, or maybe it was meant to be.

Carraigulla was an area, practically a wilderness and yet a

postal district, sitting at an elevation of six-hundred feet above sea level on the south-side of the Derrynasaggart Mountains. Acres of abandoned farmland were surrounded by square kilometers of forestry that held a hand-full of cottages inhabited by old people, one of which was empty; the local gossip had proved correct. My relief was palpable, the dream, the search had almost been realized. The stress had been beginning to build on Hilda's face as October had approached, the children were amused yet unaware and looking dazed. I was starting to feel manic. But here just off the mountain road next to a stream stood our potential home, an empty cottage encircled by trees, beyond the garden a field and a distant view of a valley and mountains. I knew the place was mine, a feeling resonated within me, I felt confident, sure to the point of certainty, yet with a degree of insanity, my new family was but an appendage, the land here was part of myself. We traced the owner easily, by drinking in the local village pubs, although this time we had to probe deeper. Yet Hilda proved her worth and the children in their innocence were effective in persuading local folks' minds to release information and even build a village fervor around our needs.

I got in touch with my 'new' landlord, he is called Steven and a dairy farmer. He seems a down-to-earth man, I can see this in his eyes and hands. The cottage has been vacant for some time, an unexpected gain from a dead uncle who was a Catholic priest and wanted somewhere to retire to near his family. The place has an eccentric air, built by the Land Commission in nineteen thirty-three, the 'modernization' of it has only added to its character. The ex-owner used old church remnants as materials, so wood from old pews, hymnbook cupboards and even an arched oak back door adorn the place. With my 'instant' family I've managed to get a tenancy agreement, although confusion and uneasiness seem to cloud Steven's face. I don't care, I've got what I wanted. We now have a home.

Chapter 8

The Garden

Land is everywhere, we take it for granted undoubtedly: patches, plots, fields, swathes, nations, continents, the very thing beneath our feet. I remember my father quoting from Mark Twain: "Buy land. They've stopped making it." An educated man no doubt. The world is finite certainly, yet as a race we continually multiply. And the issue of land and land use remains uncertain. Landscapes, geographical features, perspective, depth, color and ambiance were all considerations I took seriously when creating a composition at college. However I have read of men as artists sprinting through galleries as a performance. Japanese artists eating red paint and shitting out dye on white paper to represent the "true colonial idealism". What they are trying to communicate is the idea of space and how as a race we use and used it. Land represents and perhaps is our identity, a necessity for our future, a mother from our past. I loved my family's garden, I took the privacy and beauty for granted. After I left home I accepted the fact that I could travel freely through the landscape without care or love. Industrial terrain, ill conceived housing developments, and ugly urban planning never bothered my mind as I could move on. I finally wanted to own land in Ireland, like a man who had seen and experienced life I finally wanted to commit and marry. I fell in love with my surroundings, I was intoxicated with them. I wanted to whisper sweet promises, dote and pamper on my new companion. I wanted that fertility to impregnate my ideas, feelings and life on. I had finally found a place I wanted to stay.

Yet I discovered myself in a strange situation, everything I did was connected to the land, my work revolved around it. Any personal alliance was joined to this setting, it seemed my every move had a double meaning. My wife and her children never fell into this trap, or so I imagined, their relationships always excluded or transcended this 'predicament'. I was beholden to their emotions in attracting true and genuine friends to ourselves, because I on the other hand only seemed to attract things, objects that we wanted. Undoubtedly these goods were needed for our general benefit but their importance was somehow way above any true friendship. It appeared the need and any acquaintance were combined and the 'sad' fact was once I had acquired what I wanted the companionship was demoted. Therefore I relied on my adopted family for any real continual contact with local people. Hilda seemed to have a knack of attracting sincere friends, her children also managed this, yet I did not and did not care. For my new family offered a buffer between myself and the outside world. Maybe they even influenced others in their dealings with me, causing strangers to be more generous and courteous in their interactions, and through this I gained what I needed and what my family needed. In this way I got to know people in the area and slowly they got to know me.

With the family living off welfare I got by with odd jobs, cutting wood for the open fire and eventually gardening, consequently I spent a lot of time outdoors. Painting had turned into a hobby for the time being, it was just too impractical as a money earner in this new locale. My landlord had kindly offered me a 'small portion' of his field at the rear of the cottage which was overgrown with brambles and nettles. The actual area was quite large really, but then everything is relative. Steven had a big Massey-Ferguson tractor, I had a spade. I wasn't about to complain though, I have always loved the idea of cultivation. I love the soil, I love the land, I really don't know why. I dug the whole garden by hand and enjoyed every minute of it. In the evening I studied books about gardening and plants by the fire. The key to good gardening was fertilizer apparently, I chose natural ones. Hey shit was free. Living in an agricultural community I found out animal wastes were a problem, so pig shit, sheep shit, cow shit and horse shit were everywhere and easily available. All I had to do was ask and the farmer would deliver the stuff. I chose horse manure in the end, it was dry, mixed with straw and comparatively innocuous even when fresh. Besides I adored horses and now worked occasionally at a stable yard.

Over time the garden grew: apple, pear and cherry trees were added, perennial shrubs, flowers and vegetables and even a hive of bees. One night in May I decided to go for a slug patrol. A little joke on my part, yet slugs eat young plants as any gardener knows. Being an organic gardener and of a certain nature, I collected them from my garden and transferred them to other areas, usually on the other side of the stream as they are strangely territorial. A paradise was outside my back door, cultivated land meeting wild, the boundary was indeterminate and relative. Nettles are edible. The moon was full and over the pine and hardwood trees that claimed the brook's banks. Stripes of black and silver traversed the plot. The beehive reverberated, the sound filling the sultry night air, along with the overpowering scent of honey; bees never rest when the weather is fine. The whole scene was bewitching to the point of lunacy. There is a medieval woodcut that shows rural villages and a landscape at night, a vagabond or peasant has wandered across the scene. He reaches the horizon and peers behind it, spying on the mechanisms behind reality: the great cog wheels, gears and ratchets that control the heavens and earth. This is how *I* felt that night collecting slugs.

At the back of the cottage was a stream. It almost literally cascaded past my back door, I could hear it at night, a background of white noise from the whitewater. Occasionally in the summer, if the weather was continually hot and dry it would be reduced to a trickle. The mountain road passed here and a long time ago someone had built a ford, when it was constructed I couldn't really tell or find out, but since the gradient of the stream was steep the builders had used natural rock to make a level passing place, giving birth to a waterfall. As a beautiful unintended spin-off one really had to study the feature to see it was artificial. Much much later when the common grazing land on the mountain above was taken from the people and converted to forestry, overseen by a quasi government department, the ford was converted to a bridge and large artless concrete pipes had been laid across it, with a layer of tarmac on top. Ireland was ever practical, poverty had bred pragmatism.

Now articulated lorries thundered over it with Nature's selfless bounty; tons of wood on its way to be pulped so I and others could wipe our arses in comfort. Regardless of this, another odd feature that was apparent if one looked carefully was a water channel, it was natural looking yet obviously artificial. Built by some genius it left the main body of the stream on a neighbor's land crossed under the road, snaking across the fields providing a distinct boundary. Whoever had built it had been fiendishly clever as they had followed the natural contours of the land, so the result was it flowed as an ordinary river does, the banks that housed it planted with willow, ash and alder. For myself the effect was stunning, even though it was man-made, the reality was truly practical and beautiful. So I consulted Joe a neighbor on the issue on why and when it had been constructed. The first part of the answer was obvious, the waterway was for watering the cattle and irrigation in various fields and yards as it made its way to the river. He nodded at my silence misinterpreting my wonder for ignorance. I had to repeat the second part, yet he waved his hand away dismissively and said it had always been there, as though God had created it. I chose not to comment and returned to my garden.

Digging one day and planning to construct a greenhouse, I

contemplated the idea of irrigation. It seemed I was inspired by the builders of the channel. If I took a bucket with a mesh on top and fastened a hose to a hole in the bottom of it, then placed it far enough 'upstream' in the channel, I would have a gravity feed system, a constant free supply of water for my garden during the summer months. No power costs or bills. Nature would provide the water with a natural free force. So I bought a length of hose and laid it in the artificial waterway, as using the stream itself would have been ridiculous considering flash floods and the strong current.

However the pipe was so long it had to cross the road somehow, also a higher elevation was needed for greater pressure. Still where the channel met the real water course was a mystery, I'd presumed it passed under the road somewhere and connected to it on a neighbor's property. I had to find the source. Therefore I began beating through the undergrowth and shrubs searching and eventually I found an entrance to a narrow tunnel, something I had never noticed before. What now? The only solution was to grab the end of the hose and crawl through it. I crouched in my Wellingtons and started to inch forward letting my eyes adjust to the dim light, pushing away thoughts of claustrophobia. My figure almost filled the gap, plugging the entrance so to speak, only the water was left trickling under my boots. The reflected light glazed the ceiling creating a tomb like effect all in tonal grays, as if I was creeping into an engraving. A few minutes passed and the perspective became more apparent: a series of cut stones with chiseled joints, like a miniature medieval church ceiling, ran to the far end of the passage, where bright light and water poured through an aperture.

Thirty ton trucks rumbled over this everyday and no one knew or no one cared. I stepped forward awkwardly dragging my other foot behind. The stream this channel connected with flowed into a river two hundred feet below in the valley floor and up river from the local village two stone towers stood.

Both were privately owned now. I took another clumsy step. The northern fortress had been converted into a beautiful yet freakish family home, the southern one had been left in its original state. I shuffled forward again. While listening to local gossip at the stable yard the owner mentioned that a small repair job done on the battlements had revealed an odd facsimile of the builder's face and the date fifteen-fourteen carved into the stone. I kept moving. Ireland had been invaded centuries ago and mile upon mile of forest that hid the Gaelic kingdoms had been chopped down. The intruders had chosen the best ground to occupy, clear and dominate. The stone towers were sentinels from the past. The land was to be tamed. I reached the end of the passage and looked up through a carved stone grate, feeling like a prisoner. I pushed the hose through, then made a difficult turn and scampered back as fast as possible, caring not about wetting my clothes.

Hilda and the children took an interest in my activities, yet the garden was really mine. It was my backdoor escape from ordinary life, a passion that became an obsession. A mental addiction, a physical ecstasy, a total preoccupation, a secret lover. Hilda sprouted her own interests with neighbors and her family, and the children grew like my garden, but akin to flowers growing in their beds they were really connected to their mother. I was just an overseer, sometimes a beloved servant, someone who was a stand-in that fitted into the required role, but never actually filled the position authentically. As time passed I became a Puck like figure creeping in the back door at dusk with my fruit and vegetables.

Chapter 9

Growing Dinners

I grew a dinner once. I decided the land and my handiwork would produce an entire meal. For most people living in the first world nations food is ubiquitous, even a problem: saturated and unsaturated fats, calories and sugar content. God how we hate it. Dieting has spawned a new industry. For others living in lesser circumstances it is a problem as well. I wanted to grow a dinner, a complete meal from the land I cultivated.

Feeding is more than our physical diet and I was nourishing more than my physical body with my garden. But let me speak with confidence in my ignorance, I relate stories of the land, the nuances in nature blossoming in my mind. I was trying to create an interconnected landscape, a natural habitat for myself where I was joined to the whole, where I could gather the bounty with the minimal effort and input. The initial work would be intense, but as the system integrated I would hypothetically have to spend less time and effort in giving and have more time for leisure and harvesting. Most animals browse, even scientists say hunter gatherers in the right type of landscape took less than three hours for foraging, same with dolphins apparently, they spend a lot of time playing. I wanted that reality and I was intelligent enough to understand it was a possibility. This principle, this theory became a preoccupation relegating even my family and neighbors to mere accessories, to minor parts in the great scheme I was creating. And only the choicest was to be chosen to join me in my new kingdom. In spite of this aloofness and detachment, Hilda and the children continued to introduce local people into my life: Joe and his sister who were neighbors, John a local farmer and his parents. Noel and his wife, environmentalists from the nearby town. A community organic gardeners group. Yet they were just faces passing through my life, secondary figures who might give me clues to the magnificent natural domain I was building. Otherwise everyone became just an obstacle I had to placate so I could return to my real endeavor. I was designing a new Eden and unconsciously crowning my new Eve. People were irrelevant, my own family included.

I accepted the everyday chores like taking the children to school, shopping and doing odd jobs around the house. Socially I fell in with my wife's wishes in meeting new friends and a network of neighbors. But above this I had my own mental landscape disconnected from others' suppositions, whatever I encountered I played along with, meanwhile writing another narrative in my head. Reality did not affect me as I had my own developing embryonic scenario. I felt beyond all mundane affairs and though I became involved in others' lives, their conversations, attachments and allegiances meant nothing when I returned to my garden. It seemed I had transcended the petty problems people encounter, the trivialities of life, the garbage that sheer existence sometimes throws at us. I was immune to it and I *knew* all the answers. I was patiently working on my piece of land, slowly connecting all the disparate parts together into one glorious holistic whole, and while I did it my lucid mind could see the solutions to all others' boring, banal, and silly, predicaments, issues and troubles. However I was enlightened enough to not usually become involved, I was intelligent enough not to offer advice most of the time.

To be completely honest I was really unconcerned. Picking raspberries early one summer morning with the dew and the coolness of dawn wrapped around my body I felt like a bear, indeed it was only later when I returned to the cottage did the feeling register. At the time the low early sun was glancing off the foliage, the lazy drone of bees was around, munching with contentment my hands reached out automatically, juice running down my chin. Hunkered down between the canes aroused yet satisfied with the earthy scents filling my nostrils, birds were twittering and singing, daring to share my meal, hopping through the long grass and over the mulch.

Unfortunately Hilda had plans of her own: the grass needed to be cut, a lawnmower was required. The bees were a danger to her and the children. The trees blocked the light from the cottage and had to be felled. I sensed I was an ape losing its habitat, but I knew for certain these complaints were just pointers to something else. The processes and functions that they were attached to were changing and hastening to a time where the late summer of her life would bear a different fruit. I chose to soothe and pacify, as from my experience with my garden I knew the whole situation was a natural one. This was my terrible confidence at the time. So believing in this fact I skirted around the issues and the arguments, spending more time outdoors perfecting my vision.

A nightmare: it's dark now and I'm pushing towards the light, the tunnel has an end, I can see it. I'm wet and I slither out into the bright landscape, greens, yellows and translucent blue, the colors are almost painful. There is a breeze on my face, light and caressing. In every direction I can see trees, luminescence mottles the ground, shifting as the leaves sway in the gentle wind. I'm on the move weaving through the trunks and despite the peaceful ambiance I know evil is close by stalking, waiting for an opportune moment to grab me. An old familiar presence that wants to destroy me, that always did and continues to scheme and may forever do so. The landscape will not protect me, the trees offer no sanctuary, their own destruction is part of the same process, I am certain. As this last thought dissolves I attempt to press on, hoping to escape, praying to flee. Yet these very prayers summon the opposite and I am caught roughly and expertly in a tight grip. Fear floods my mind as pain and blackness descend upon me.

I wake up gasping and sweating.

Chapter 10

Joseph and Mary

My neighbor Joseph O'Flaherty told me a story once. He had lived all his life in the same spot. Never moved. His parents had built the house before he was born. As a child he had walked everywhere. A horse and trap had taken him to town as a young man. Now at eighty he never went anywhere, anymore, he never left the house or garden. The farm that surrounded him had grown wild, with a whole new selection of indigenous plants and trees. I viewed the 'ecosystem' out of the window, the adjoining land was the same. The area that was called Carraigulla, which meant "rock of the apple" in Gaelic, was one big unintentional nature reserve.

Obviously this general state of things was different from his childhood memories. His parents' farm had had cows and ducks and hens, a few pigs. A horse. A vegetable patch. Various small fields sown with potatoes, even oats, and a stand of apple trees that still remained near the cottage. One of which had blown down in the recent storm and I had been cutting up with my chainsaw.

Well he and his brothers and sisters had charged around the farm working and messing around. Throwing stones at the apple trees in the autumn to collect apples was one such activity. Too lazy to pick up the ladders and gleefully using the trees as target practice, rocks and stones were pelted at the fruit. Occasionally some of the stones must have wedged into the forks of branches or fallen into the hollow where the bole and the boughs met. Inevitably the tree would grow around them, encasing them in wood. My chainsaw must have hit one he chortled. The "rock of the apple" had broken my teeth.

Carraigulla was a landscape, a physical reality but its essence became a dreamscape, a state of mind. A symbolic idea that took over my conscious and unconscious psyche. I dreamed about it and still do. Carraigulla was I and I was Carraigulla.

Imagine this: acre upon acre of pasture land returning to native woodland. The old field systems were reverting back to something far more ancient and like the hands on a clock face the changes were unnoticeable. They could not be discerned in the immediate moment, but the gradual aggregation had a force that was unstoppable. Over the months and years paths had disappeared, stone walls and ruins had disintegrated, copses had enlarged and tangles of bramble and nettle had proliferated, acting as natural incubators for more saplings. All the boundaries were disappearing. The whole area was slipping back into the primeval forest humans had originally staggered from. The woods had been our womb and like a baby emerging into the world the first thing humanity had done was shat into its environment. Carraigulla was running concurrently to this. It was the opposite force and I adored it. I was witness to it. At times it felt like my private kingdom. It possessed my soul and changed my understanding of life. This is the real earth I told myself, this is nature as an expression of itself.

For sure humanity was part of it, the dominant species and as that environmental destruction almost seemed as natural as a bird crapping here in the woods. But hey believe me mature woodland is a cosmic art-form. I often wandered down by the stream at the back of my house. It was an area I never touched, hell it was an area no one had touched for five-hundred years or more. A water channel had been constructed in the early sixteenth century to conduct water across the fields. It was a natural feature now. The rest comprised of large trees, ferns, assorted plants and grasses. But if you visited the place anytime of the year I guarantee you would think there was some invisible gardener toiling away there everyday. The area was like a well kept botanical park. The first time I saw it I was puzzled, later I accepted it. Even so from time to time I wondered why it was so ordered. Therefore browsing through the local library I decided to do some research and eventually I found my answer: apparently any developed temperate woodland heads in that direction anyway, it is its natural mature state. The wild chaos of Carraigulla would one day if left alone be the same. Consequently according to the reference book I studied some genius had taken this natural phenomenon into account and designed a "forest garden". Everything in his woodland was edible. So literally all he did was wander around collecting the food, like some postmodernist ape returning to his newly constructed paradise. Back into the trees I mused. A rejoining to nature at a higher level. A loop in evolution. The idea transfixed me, it was something I had felt all along. Carraigulla became my deity. I was its resident primate. I wanted to evolve.

For Joseph this was his home, a place that was special but not profound. Ironically he might have understood it more than I did. Later I came to see him as analogous to a native aboriginal. He saw the trees as timber and as a practical man considering all aspects, they were beautiful, but they also provided fuel. I disliked the idea of cutting down living trees, besides there was so much deadwood around I considered it unnecessary.

One afternoon he asked me if I could fell a large ash tree next to his house. Ash he explained burned green and the distance carrying it indoors would be minimal. I contemplated the request. The labor was inconsequential to me. And any payment made by Joe was usually meager but I didn't mind. The danger I would have ignored had it been dead, it was listing towards the house though. What disturbed my mind the most was it was alive, almost mature and really beautiful. I tried to dissuade him and being aware of his nature I said it was far too risky considering it was perceptively leaning towards his cottage. The top mass of branches and leaves were insignificant, any sane person could see there was no real counter weight of twigs and foliage that might pull the tree in the opposite direction. I used this as an excuse to hide my true feelings. The logic of my argument struck him, I could see he was ruminating on what I had said, but the force of my belief was absent. I wasn't really concerned. The tree was alive and no way was I going to do the wicked deed. He must have seen my lack of anxiety figuring I was confident, but just too lazy to help. I said goodbye and wandered back home.

Working in my garden other realities burgeoned in my mind. I was not trained to use a chainsaw. I had just gone out and bought one from a local store. One slip and the house really could be destroyed or severely damaged. Then again Joe and Mary were old people who relied on me and trusted me to help them. And yes they did need fuel to keep them warm, to cook and heat water. Weeks passed and the ethics of the task effortlessly revolved in my mind until one morning Joe called at my door. This was a freakish and unusual occurrence. After a brief intro of what a beautiful day it was he came straight to the point. The ash tree. He needed the fuel. He would pay me extra. He pleaded and begged. I had to give in. I told him the extra money was unnecessary and looked around morosely at the beautiful May day. He was correct in that it was clear and fine, cool in the shadows and warm in the sun. We walked down the lane towards his cottage silently. He self-conscious but happy, I now lost in thoughts of danger.

A slow terror was now creeping up on me, the tree was large, massive even. I had been so wrapped up in my principles and love of nature the dilemma had been no more than a theoretical problem. Carraigulla had indeed entered my mind and taken over. Roots had grown into my brain, fronds had embraced and slowly enveloped me, their tendrils entwining my soul. I might have been contemplating the murder of a family member. I thoroughly disagreed with the idea, but his pleading had been wretched, so I had given in.

The ash loomed above the cottage like gigantic amiable friend protecting a small acquaintance. There was not a breath of wind. I felt inconsolable. The terror had dissipated to be replaced by despair. I hoped the tree might crush myself and Joe to death. When I started the saw it brought to mind executioners placing blindfolds on prisoners. I began my act of murder. I used textbook cuts, my real experience at felling large trees was practically nil. The chainsaw had a long bar so I nicked out a reasonably large wedge from the 'back' of the tree, towards the base. This was the direction I intended it to fall. The top cut was horizontal, the bottom was inclined. The wedge dropped out perfectly, I might have well been demonstrating for Stihl. The books usually suggested the cut be a third of a diameter of the trunk. Mine was slightly under that and for a fraction of a second I was glad in some far off abstract realm, as ash is notorious for splitting suddenly. I moved to the 'front' working like an automaton. Articles I had read on such things generally said: hold the saw at an angle and make the final downward diagonal cut to almost meet the open wedge on the opposite side of the trunk.

If I have described it accurately, you'll get the general idea. The whole operation encourages the tree to fall in the desired direction as the notch slowly closes, as the tree topples. Unfortunately things can go amiss for professionals and idiots like myself. I felt uncomfortable. What was also disconcerting was that Joe was standing almost directly behind me watching the whole procedure. I occasionally caught his beaming face out of my peripheral vision. The tree was big, the chainsaw bar was somewhat smaller than the diameter of the trunk and I in a macho state of mind had purchased a twenty-four inch bar. As I slowly let the revolving chain eat through the wood, I thought this is it. However, the tree gripped the saw slightly and the motor coughed. I felt extremely cold as though death was actually stalking me. But this was just a feeling. The intelligent thought arrived a couple of seconds later: the wood was nipping the chain, the tree was falling towards the house. I remember the panic and looking up at the high branches distorted by perspective. I managed to pull out the saw and push Joe away. Silently we both gazed upward, he was oblivious still grinning, I was terrified. The tree remained motionless. Out of nowhere a strong breeze picked up. You never really hear the wind it's the things it touches that make the noise. All the leaves acted like streamers, pennants. It was a blessing. Banners at a festival. Slowly and majestically it fell exactly where Joe had pointed earlier. For the rest of the day I kept looking for more breezes. I would stop working, still feeling in shock and glance around pensively searching for evidence of a wind, but everything remained motionless. The remainder of the day was completely still.

That night I sat in front of the open fire contemplating so-called reality. And the supernatural. Our minds are an interior landscape. Our own personal space. How did they connect with the larger perceived reality? This was a mystery. I had had various theories about consciousness and reality in the past, but really I was talking pat. How could the fortuitous breeze be explained, conjured out of nowhere. Perhaps Joe was more in touch with the 'real' reality than I was. Perhaps his Catholic upbringing induced him to pray, I don't know. He certainly had been inspired. We both had been. We had chosen the exact time to pull off the deed successfully. Our thoughts and actions had dovetailed into the greater scheme of things and produced a successful result. I had dismissed the idea that the wind had been created just for us. Joe might have thought differently. If cornered into answering such a query he might have mentioned the fairies, but to be honest I don't think he believed in such things. Or the 'Banshee' for that matter. For him these subjects were to be treated with wide-eyed mocking after some rum toddies. The real truth was Joe was a simple man in some respects. I'm not saying he lacked intellect he just accepted certain things. "The breeze had come at the right time. Providence had been blessed upon us and no more than that. Good men were looked after." Maybe he closed his eyes and clasped his hands that night, mumbling his prayers and saying thanks for the wood. But certainly the next day the whole episode would be forgotten and labeled just another day. Joe's strength was that he loved me, I could see it in his face. I liked him, I loved Carraigulla. I think all our loving thoughts kept the place unsullied. It was our private paradise. When my family collapsed because of the break-up with my wife. When Joe died and his sister was taken away to live with a relative. When I finally lost my mind and ran away from Ireland forever, Carraigulla was dismantled. The land was sold, the beautiful woods uprooted and burned. All one-hundred acres turned into three vast empty fields. My Carraigulla remains in my soul. I dream about it. But now the visions are peaceful, and unfortunately symbolic I guess. I finally understood its message. Alas I am Carraigulla. So no matter where I am in the world, if there is any true peace in my life, my night time dreams reflect this contentment as I wander through the cool dappled woods.

Chapter 11

Going mad at Carraigulla.

"She's left you asshole."
I bury my head in my hands.
"Left you, left you, left you."
My eyes water.
"Ha ha ha ha ha."
I've got to get to a friend. Maybe Noel.
"Noel is a demon from another planet."
I must explain my situation.
"Tell him we are in control."
I begin to weep.
"Hey big boy don't cry, we'll look after you."
I submit.

A sense of emptiness, yet safety pervades my feelings. The warm early summer afternoon passes by with a profound inevitability. (If fully) analyzed any moment reveals either complete utter desolation or minutiae that are so relevant they border on the esoteric. A godlike view from a madman. There is no routine to follow now, nothing from the past is relevant to my life. Something is dictating different orders to me in my mind. Certain new procedures must be followed. Another day. The next day? I am eating pizza outside a shop and a familiar face passes by. I think he wants to start a conversation, but after glimpsing at my hands he hurries away. I am not upset. I stare at my hands.

They are black with dirt and soot. The nails are long, curled and filthy. I have never noticed this before, perhaps I should cut them. This thought registers strongly in my consciousness. It repeats in a loop. Over and over again. I laugh at the obvious. It is late summer now and I am ingrained with dirt and stink. Where have I been? It appears my mind has been occupied in other realms. I feel I have been invaded and possessed. I have memories but they are confused and surreal. Thought is contagious I think. I am in a local town at present, the local town I frequented so much before with my family. I have been greeted by a person I haven't seen for some time. Someone my wife introduced me to. Noel. I just picked up his disgust at my condition. Yet what have I been doing to be in such a state? Hilda and the children have been gone for a while. Where have I been? A voice reminds me, speaking in my head.

Blue and white up. Green and yellow down. Fresh and sweet. Soft and verdant. Lush. Then a coarse and rough texture my fingers can caress, I wrap my arms around the bole and hunker down to feel the soil below. Raw umber, burnt sienna, ocher, earthy and moist, silica glowing. But now for action, 'Herne' tells me to follow and I obey trotting into the woods. Barefoot. Spikes pierce at the entrance. A little test. Are the voices tittering? Through the bramble and onwards. Light and dark, light, dark, light, dark, light, dark. I break into a run. I'm going the right way; 'Herne' is beckoning downhill towards the river. It's a test and I will prove I am man enough.
"Do the thorns and nettle stings feel good?"
Yes I nod my head in agreement
"I knew you would pass big boy."
The brook is between the trees glittering. I know what I must do. I must try to pass this new trial and even though my body will ache I know I will be rewarded.

I'm very wet and my body smarts but I think I have succeeded. But for now I must... There is a noise and movement. A bird flaps away through the broken bands of shadow and light that crisscross the wooded incline, the sun is lower in the sky dazzling my eyes. Is that 'Herne' flitting from trunk to trunk? I swear it is. I've caught him out of the corner of my eye. Yes I'm sure it is. He says he is my leader and I have lots to learn. He speaks in my mind and tells me to look to my dreams. Last night I was walking down this same sunny slope with three fat pigs, I carried a stick and had to shout and wave the staff to guide them. Marching through the soft mulch I knew the day was good, yet a sense of times past suffuses the vision. The pigs are my wife and her children and the old evolutionary triangle of food, sex and aggression are evident. The earth communicates this truth. I was in control, the feeling of power and appetite impregnate the dream, an analogy to my recent thoughts on life and sexuality vibrating in my lizard-mammalian brain. How often we devolve. The earth is a mother of sorts that needs respect or so 'Herne' tells me. Yet a mother who might eat her own children.

Another day. Bright light in my face.
"Follow the instructions and start chanting: 'foot and mouth is about. It has broken out. People will catch the disease. It's been following in your footsteps with ease. Walking right behind you.' Now you must hold the candles apart and slowly bring them together chanting all the while. Come on fucker repeat the incantation. 'Foot and mouth is about...' "

"Okay how about this fucker: 'your hominid baby bones are buried beneath the boards' Ha ha almost a tongue twister. After escaping from 'the garden' with mummy all those millenniums ago someone had an accident didn't he? Ahh poor baby. And mummy loped away."

"Hey the Prince of Darkness only wants to get close to you."
"But little one it's not about evil it's about knowledge."

I'm woken up from a dream.
"Come little one I'm here to help you."
My body is invaded and my tired limbs are possessed. I feel like a puppet. A force occupies my flesh. The friendly voice continues telling me certain jobs need to be done. I am flung off the sofa and onto my feet. Clomp, clomp, clomp, my legs

automatically stride across the floor. I am deadbeat, exhausted, my muscles have no energy, but a power keeps me upright. There is no pain, I am not fighting anything yet something is within me automating my every move and a narrative continues in my mind. I am told various tasks need my attention, but not to worry as when they are completed I may rest. Firstly my car needs some attention. I have been driving it for sure – I can't remember exactly when – a long time ago, I have vague memories of the beach and the seashore at dawn and a new moon hanging in the sky. At other times the road is dark and I am traversing mountains, jabbering away to myself, even as something else is chatting away in my mind informing me I am being followed and giving directions for my escape. There is an all consuming feeling of paranoia swelling up. While I bounce around on the rough track gunning the accelerator, a voice starts to mock and deride me saying I am going to die.

These memories are from the time when my wife had just left and I did not sleep. But now I'm outside on the footpath and the bright sunlight is stinging my eyes. I forgot it was mid morning – the front room of the cottage is gloomy with the wooden shutters tightly closed. I'm blinking confused but then the voice continues.

"But little one we must put water in the car."

I obey, but I still don't seem to have control over my limbs, as I hop and skip to the outside tap, filling an old large gallon can. I pirouette like a marionette and bounce towards my car. There is something bright red and large in front of me, I'm not sure. I'm exhausted and must sleep, yet it seems every time I close my eyes I've been awakened to perform a task. For example meals must be prepared and cooked with absolute precision with the correct ingredients. Sometimes as I do things there is chanting in my head. My hands automatically reach for the the bonnet release and pour water into the radiator, it almost takes half the can. I slam the bonnet shut and stare at my car, my red car.

"Now to the chicken little one."
The chicken? I'm marched off into the garden and field legs snapping like scissors. There is a box in the middle of the field, a wooden box. I made it. It has wire mesh on it and a door. I open it and a bedraggled chicken flies out. I'm sure there were more. Anyway apparently I may rest now.

A strange dream: Studying a picture I finally understand the meaning of Darkness and Light. Surely you all think darkness is evil and goodness is light. We have metaphors all over our language that attest to this theory. But please examine these two conditions closely. Do not these two states only represent equal opposites, say the darkness representing a denseness, a compactness or compression and the light its counter, an airiness, a form of expansion? Consider the colors, if pigments are mixed together fully and completely do they not offer a dullness? Yet is this fact an ignorance or even evil? I propose the Darkness symbolizes no more than a closeness and the Light represents no more than a distance. Is not then the Darkness as true as the Light? Does not the Darkness require a passion? Does not the Light require a detachment? Hence either may accommodate the wicked or the worthy. Therefore please consider the following aspects: divine, angelic, demonic and satanic. These are far more relevant. They represent unconscious good, conscious good, unconscious evil, and conscious evil. The question of how close any of us are to the said conditions determines the lightness and darkness of one's soul.

I wake up confused with the line "Another message from Durer," echoing in my head. I feel this information is important and somehow I am being helped.

Chapter 12

The madness continues

A so-called friend had left a message on my answering service, his worried voice had been caught in a loop in my electronic mailbox. He wanted to visit to make sure I was alright. I knew he was lying though, I knew he was insincere. The voices had told me so. He had even confessed to his deceitfulness in my mind. This scenario was similar to other encounters I had experienced before. Some time earlier another friend had been revealed as he truly was. His identity had become clear as a Satanic being that had obvious intentions to harm me. I had picked up his thought patterns. Fortunately I had been advised at the time. A clear calm voice had told me what to do and I had made my escape. This was a comparable situation and therefore I had to leave the safety of Carraigulla as he would be arriving soon. There was one place I might elude him and be safe, a neighbor who was Divine. I quickly drove down the mountain road to his farm hoping for a clean escape, I wanted to avoid any detection. John was in his yard as usual so I smiled and waved through the windscreen as I parked my car. He just nodded seemingly indifferent, not that this gesture worried me in any way. I had been advised before that his status was generally Divine.

To be truly aware and Angelic was a rare thing. Typically people were either Divine or Demonic in their dealings with their daily lives as these attitudes had grown out of millions of years of soul evolution and since the vast majority of this time had been spent as animals, all feelings were therefore unconscious. The voices had specifically stated that our everyday normal temperaments had developed from this time period. Consequently solid reliable goodness was as steady as generations of herbivores and their young chewing cud over the eons. We had been such things long before evolution had marched us into this modern phase of humanity. I opened the door and got out of my car. John blinked in surprise at my unannounced arrival, uncertain of what to say.

My plan was to stay all afternoon and evening to avoid any confrontation with my unwelcome visitor. And anyway John had a good nature and never seemed to mind any intrusion and occasionally I would help him with odd jobs and get paid. The farm that he worked on belonged to his parents whom he lived with, one day he would inherit it. So I instinctively held the gate he was welding and then we went in the house for tea. His mother Margaret welcomed me in insisting I had something to eat, his father Tim popped his head around the kitchen door to say hello and chat about his horses. There was an overwhelming feeling of coziness and amiability. This had always been the case ever since the first day I had met them. The whole parish was blessed with a Divine spirit, it pervaded the whole area.

The opposite was true of the local town, a Demonic air hung around the dole office, the pubs and the betting shops, the feeling was one of animosity and unstated but definite hostility. Satanic specters of violence, anger and cruelty clung to the huge morass of unconscious evil, feeding from it. To walk through it was to immerse oneself in a battery of thought forms created since life began. A block of energy vibrating with negativity which was mostly unaware but spawned seeds of cognizant force that infected people's minds and encouraged conscious evil deeds. The very earth itself reverberated with this power as epochs had elapsed and various life forms had continually passed migrating and charged up the matter around them with a negative or positive spin. Various cultures called these lines lay lines, energy lines or dragon lines, but I knew the real truth as the voices had told me where they had originated from. Thought energy from over a thousand millenniums of life had created these power points and demarcations, ultimately ourselves and our fellow creatures as we had evolved. As I sat in John's kitchen I contemplated all this and pondered on whether in the past his mother had been a brachiosaurus or a brontosaurus in most of her incarnations.

It was late, time must have slipped by. Margaret brought me out of my reverie with an offer of supper, but first the cows had to be milked, so naturally I offered to help. I strode out into the evening with John, feeling satisfied. How many times had I passed this way in various guises I mused? The very atoms of my body resonated with my surroundings, both were really part of each other, actually the same thing. This attraction had really guided me here, it was an inevitability that every one of us experienced but was ignorant of. Destiny was involved with both matter and consciousness evolving together, and as sentient beings we were connected to both. Oh the profound knowledge I had been given! My abstractions were interrupted by the sound of a vehicle entering the yard. John and I left the milking shed to investigate. A small Toyota car was parked adjacent to the tractor, my Satanic friend grinning behind the steering wheel. At certain times in our lives it is our reactions and physical responses that reveal our true feelings. I moved to the side of the car and purposely stood in front of the driver's door, signaling to John that all was well and I would deal with the 'unknown' visitor.

He gave an uneasy smile and started to return to the cows. The driver's window was slowly wound down and a dread set in my mind, John hesitated at the parlor door not sure if he was doing the right thing. The silence was broken with my 'old friend' greeting me, which satisfied John's curiosity as he saluted us both and went back to work. I now somehow had to get rid of this intruder, the voices had specifically stated that he was dangerous. We exchanged pleasantries for a while yet I remained blocking the car door from opening and eventually the conversation became strained. Suddenly a message was transmitted into my head giving instructions of what to say, but with my own panic and the chatter from the car's occupant I forgot the advice being channeled and the previous patter of conversation. Feeling confused and bereft of direction I looked around for a place to hide. A light pressure brought me back into the present. The car door was opening and my fear started to mount, I had to get away so I ran.

Margaret's eyes were looking intently into mine, they were full of concern, yet docile, tender and sublime. Innocent and gentle like the cows in the barn. Umber akin to the earth. Yet chocolate sweet. A sudden noise percolated the air around me and the back of Margaret's head came into view as her voice sang out an offer for coffee. A general assent was returned as I slowly turned only to be greeted by three pairs of eyes, friendly no doubt but quizzical. My so-called friend sat at the table, with John and his father. I backed away smiling and opening the door made my escape, running through the yard, on my way back to Carraigulla, I heard their voices shouting, screaming in my mind.

Chapter 13

My new reality

When my wife left Carraigulla for good I knew I became truly mad. Hearing voices, experiencing visions, and peculiar dreams, being invaded and animated by unknown forces is nothing but real insanity. I lost time and my own sense of self. Suffered from insomnia and subsequently blacked out. The feeling of fear was insurmountable. Voices chattered in my mind. Chanting, cackling and whispering mockeries. Occasionally flashes of the past bloom: seascapes at dawn, moons above forests and dark mountain roads, but in all of these scenarios I'm fleeing as something is pursuing me. It seems that advice is given directly into my head on the means of escape, but the foulness is always not far away and it creeps in too snickering at my escapades, for it already knows my moves and has time to wait and snare me. Sometimes a clear calm voice gives me inspiration, hope and perhaps love. Therefore I cling to this, it becomes my teacher, my mentor, my advisor. Simple clear facts about universal law are laid out before my bare raped mind.

I crave its commentary, its company. A protector and deity dwells in my head and I constantly await its instructions. It reveals its cosmic wisdom to me and offers advice on all matters. Through this alliance of love and respect I am strengthened and have better resolve to fight the mockers and evil that enter my brain to destroy me. Much much later I reject everything. Ironically the very presence that gave me the capacity to survive induced its own demise. I came to realize for sure that I had developed paranoia schizophrenia, and any voice or strong feelings of importance or paranoia were just delusional, just symptoms of the condition. Sardonically the voices wholeheartedly agreed and added that psychic ability could be described as practically the same thing if only a little more subtle. What is one to believe? For now, for sanity and logic's sake I consider any voice is a shattered part of my psyche. But who is to say for certain, for what are the boundaries of consciousness, I'm sure we all have our own theories. All I can say is that I must have suffered some kind of brain damage as a child, indeed I do have a cavity on the left-hand side of the top of my skull. Some accident I suppose. I have asked believe me and I always get the same answer, but it's something I'd rather not go into at the moment. Actually if I ask any question I always get a reply, but whether it's the truth or a bogus retort, I never know. Sometimes the truth comes willingly when we least expect it, so perhaps your thoughts are analogous to your children who vie for your attention. Then children can be full of wisdom as you surely know.

I will tell you more as this is a confession. There is a reason I split up with my wife. It was the very cause of my eventual ruin and later rebirth that I've been relating.

The problem that gave rise to the condition goes back to my early childhood as I mentioned before, but maybe it goes back further if certain things are to believed, although that is mere speculation and faith founded on logic rather than anything inherently true or real. Nonetheless voices whisper in my mind telling me secrets and convincing tales that interlock with so much symmetry they seem plausible. Delusions? We often think we know what reality is and what is fantasy, but do we really? They also remind me about an engraving by Durer and what it rightly means.

But back to the beginning, I have and have had obsessions, whether they are common or not I'm ignorant in knowing, I would have to be a professor to be proved, but using my common sense, I guess we all suffer from such things from time to time. Please do not be hypocritical in your judgment, let's not tut tut with mock shock at anything I disclose. What goes on in the minds of most people is rarely what we see in public, hence the cause of a lot of suffering or so I'm told. Any foul intentions or hatred always return to the owner. Our thoughts are our offspring that need to be cultivated and disciplined. I know this for certain as mine murmur in my mind, but then admittedly life is a mystery.

There is a freshness to the land here and I have a strong attraction to the area as you know. Digging in the garden is like cutting into a huge cake, the bounty of food growing is such a simple idea, it almost seems ridiculous. Most people associate food with supermarket shelves rather than the soil. The succulence of the plants, the fragrance of the flowers, the bees and the butterflies programmed to do their tasks – animated specs of color. My garden is a living entity, I collect my breakfast from it during the summer months, for dinner I run out the back door with a spade. It is mine and I love it. Trees and a brook border it on one side, beyond the fence grow plantains, thistles and banks of nettles, all edible plants waiting for my plate, free salads from creation. In the woods I tiptoe as ferns, bracken, heather and saplings litter the ground, huge trunks soar above my head, I'm walking in a living incubator of life. I cut down dead trees planning my every move intricately, as each life form squashed is a defeat. I crave the fecundity of life. Its beauty and innocence always needs protection, we must not pervert the pure. Yet as a species we knowingly abuse the land. Confidently we destroy life. Our cities and our culture dominate the landscape, proliferating beyond any natural control. I see the lunacy of such things and in contrast the simplicity of nature. But I have fallen into a comparable trap as a terrible analogy has appeared in my life, and I have become caught and seduced all of my own making. Everything I do and act is a prevarication, as I have ignored the most important aspects of my life, ignorantly worrying about insignificant details which have no bearing on this reality. I am complicit with my thoughts, I have been incompetent in dealing with them and let them evolve without hindrance, even encouraging their propagation. A conspiracy against my wife has germinated, matured and ripened. I pose in my own thought scape that runs contrary to those whom I should truly love and protect, and strangely their dreams reflect this pathetic stance, yet these nightmares remain unrecognized for what they are. This obsession I hide controls me more each day. I am living a lie and I hate myself, my desires and my existence. I have spawned animosity, malice and distrust in others I originally loved. Wittingly I dissolved the bonds with my wife for I had seen my stepdaughter's face framed by apple blossom.

Is the unconscious conscious? Are there entities living in the mind scapes of life? Hatching out from our creative processes. Flitting undetected from being to being. Surreal ethereal angels and devils. A creative thought form universe.

Chapter 14

Summer 2008

I'm at a stop light and it's hot as hell as usual. My mind is bombarded with concepts and the occasional voice taunting me, a regular occurrence in this type of situation I suppose. Sometimes I snarl back, sometimes I pray, I guess the latter is better, I've been advised it is anyway. I've got my own theories but I'm still never really sure what controls these dialogs, I'm told it's me apparently. Whatever, I'm technically raving mad and teaching business and conversational English in Taiwan. Yet I think the madness is outside myself, the voices I can just about cope with. Shit, they sometimes even translate Chinese for me. It's this reality that is my lunacy now and what I yearn to escape from. The traffic is thick as usual, with mile after square mile of baking concrete and tarmac, hundreds of thousands of people are on the move, the air quality sucks.

Shops are chock full of goods and an army of sales people awaits, fans and air conditioners humming, some with their doors open in a gesture of invitation. Beyond the commercial district factories and huge industrial parks operate continuously, never closing, twenty-four hours a day they are churning out goods for our consumption. Yesterday my last conversation class topic was the great Pacific garbage patch: two areas of garbage and waste four to five times the size of Germany float one hundred meters thick in the doldrums of the Pacific Ocean, every piece of shit that was ever lost or thrown into the sea seemingly ends up there. I watched a CNN report on cable TV, the ice is melting at the poles, a berg ten times the size of Manhattan Island has broken away from Antarctica and it's nearly mid-May and meant to be winter down there. And according to the BBC news channel twenty-seven percent of the animals on planet Earth have disappeared in the last thirty-five years including lots of honey bees. Yet the cockroaches – up to two inches long here – crawl everywhere no matter what poison is thrown down. I race down Cheng Gong road trying to beat the lights, I know in my heart now I'm no exception, the cheesy idea that everyone makes a difference is true. I could choose to cycle which I have done so once before, sweating and gasping for air, my legs pumping and my lungs filled with exhaust fumes I cursed as some fat bitch in a three liter Mercedes broke a red light and almost totaled me. Never again. I reach my company and try to find a parking spot, scooters stretch as far as the eye can see.

This island is the most densely populated country in the world after Bangladesh apparently, the birth rate is dropping yet the new government offer incentives for low wage couples, which includes myself and my partner to marry and have children. What insanity is this? Where are we going as a race? It's a week-end and the cram school is practically empty, fuck knows how it makes a profit. The air conditioner is blasting away, in fact it is so cold inside the few students who are around are wearing sweaters and woolen jumpers. The desk girl smiles as I pass by. Feminism has not reached this part of the world yet, I can wear anything I like as a foreign teacher, but the desk staff – always young pretty women – must wear ass-tight short candy pink skirts. I clock in and dash up the stairs. New posters adorn the walls, ninety percent in Chinese, their titles written boldly in my mother tongue proudly proclaim "We are speeking Englihs." I cringe as this is a national company yet no one is paid to proof read anything. Then again this is nothing new, I downloaded a government motorcycle test only to find some of the questions incomprehensible.

The world is mad, I know I am sane. Yet I realize to hate and curse all this is negative and only enhances my pessimistic and perhaps evil emotions and thought entities that plague my mind. I must remain positive and appreciate my life and the love and respect I have found here. Today I have five students in my class and the article for discussion is about the world food crisis. Food prices have risen so fast recently that the U.N.'s predicted budget for food aid is ridiculously small. Kofi Amman the ex-secretary has said there must be a concerted effort by rich countries to feed and aid the third world, mainly Africa.

The students are polite, but unconcerned, the topic could be about anything, they have no sense of interest or passion about the subject and are woefully lacking in any knowledge about Africa, its past or current problems. They are Taiwanese and are immersed in their own culture. I remain calm, I've learned from past mistakes, I'm here to teach English and facilitate learning not start some political debate. Still I'm at a loss, the place is so insular, even though the students' intelligence and ability is amazing, their ignorance and feeling about others' lives can be appalling, but I'm generalizing. And who am I to comment on others and who they might be? I may be informed on certain issues, I may even feel strongly about these issues, yet I act not. So lately I have chosen to forget others' shortcomings and started throwing my loose change in the seven eleven donation box whenever I buy a beer after work: the guilt and the photo of the starving child spurring me to give. Perhaps this change of attitude and action turned the tumblers in consciousness and unlocked a door to further expansive thoughts. So one day after dropping my change in the African appeal box and sipping my Busch beer on a seat outside the shop, I started the usual conversation with myself.

Hey we all mind chat I guess, that is have imaginary conversations with people: real, invented, known and unknown. Well I have real voices in my head. So today I started the usual conversation and was immediately reminded of Durer's Melencholia. I coughed up my beer.

"How about the Chinese fortune tellers as well." it continued.

What has that got to do with anything? I thought.

"Hey don't you remember the message?"

The line from the engraving? Of course I do.

"And don't forget your dream."

Hey things are confusing enough for the individual let alone trying to work out patterns for the world at large. I seem to remember that two identical actions by different people can lead to completely different results due to the fact that their intentions or emotions were different.

"True enough."

So for an outsider watching such things, any model or predictable sequence is or could be impossible to discern.

"Maybe. Hey how about if we were to crawl into people's minds and find out? Spooky eh? Ha ha. We *are* your thoughts, it's a joke."

It seems to me I have animated and inflated you.

"Granted, you are us and we are you."

Hey how can I get some permanent calm in my mind? I usually have a bad time driving to work.

"We have told you before, maintain a good composure, pray away negative thought forms and emotions, even if it's in an abstract manner, it's a lot better than getting angry. Watch out for your unconscious actions when dealing with people, you tend to be unaware of things. Also watch out for the other energy centers particularly your heart, you seem to be oblivious to the activity taking place around it."

Great. Wonderful. I have to be aware twenty-four hours a day.

"Hey thought energy is like a battery. You can either charge it up or drain it away, you cannot get rid of it overnight. Obviously foreign entities clinging onto your aura might be able to be removed immediately, depending on the circumstances. But please remember this is a creative thought form universe."

So how long does it take to drain or charge up thought forms?

"Well that depends, we are really talking about an energy

envelope around you that developed from childhood. An energy body that emerged and evolved depending on your experiences and don't forget we are talking about all of the energy centers, not just your mind. A beating that you experienced as a child would not only affect your mind but your heart and other centers. And similar treatment over a long period of time would cause a very negative energy body to form."

A bitch to shift.

"Possibly."

And how about the so-called accident that caused all this?

"The event that caused the brain damage? Obviously a very traumatic episode."

I'm at the top of the stairs, a long climb but I'm steady on my feet. I can see the rich red carpet and the light blue paper on the wall of the stair head, I pat my hands on it oblivious to the fact that my mother removes my tiny hand prints each week. I'm upset and my nappy is wet, I'm a late developer. I'm on the landing now, to me it's massive and all the bedroom doors lead from it. I can hear my father humming and the bathroom floorboards creaking. I head in that direction and as I walk in the room he turns. His huge figure looms above me like an ogre. He's about to say something then chooses to ignore me. As he kneels heavily back down to sort out the clothing and towels for the airing cupboard, I start whining and continually get in his way. He keeps turning towards me and telling me to shut up and pushes me away so I get more frantic. Eventually he shoves me so hard that I topple backward striking my head on the round but hard radiator pipe.

I start screaming as the shock and pain are intense. He picks me up and tries to console me and after some time when I cease crying he lays me down on the bed and tiptoes from the room. Hours have passed or minutes and I'm dropping off to sleep, but it feels as though I am suffocating. I can't catch my breath, then suddenly I'm floating and I feel fine. I don't want to go back as I feel more complete, happier even, but something is making me.

I'm buying another beer. The accident scene is a new memory, sometimes I think it's a false one, a fabricated story invented by my mind because of the treatment metered out by my father, who was cruel and vindictive to me sometimes. I was punished severely for the slightest mistake. But permanent brain damage and a near death experience? Well I'm living proof of the first and every time I ask for the truth I get the same reply, yet the incident feels indistinct.

"Hey do you remember the quote?"

You mean the one you gave me from the magic square in Durer's Melencholia. Yeh I do.

"How about an interpretation, it's from the sixteenth century. So what about a modern context?"

Mmm, you tell me.

"Hey do you believe in destiny? Fate?"

I like to think so.

"Hey remember we are just your thought patterns and we connect to the universe at large passing through various energy centers. But remember you are really just talking to yourself."

Very funny.

"Well think about destiny, where does it truly come from? Try to be logically consistent. Compare the starving child on the donation box and yourself. How come you are drinking beer, generally healthy with a job and a girlfriend? And he is dying through lack of food and lots of his fellow Africans are dying young and old."

Hey the girlfriend is good luck?

"Okay, okay point taken. But let's take this seriously. Also I'm sure you know why she is the way she is."

I know, I know all that stuff I was told about karma.

"Yeh the old chestnut cracked. Destiny is connected to reincarnation. What you do in one life echoes into the future and many of your future incarnations. Granted we are in a creative thought form universe and there are many factions, but whatever you do you grow towards, simple logic. Matter and consciousness evolving together. Do you remember the wildlife program you saw with the mountain gorillas? Afterwards you thought the apes looked after their young better than most people. Well they do. Well better than your parents did anyhow. Imagine them evolving further and keeping their vegetarian diet. Imagine the thought forms emerging from such a vegetarian society."

Yeh, very clever but what has that got to do with Melencholia?

"Do you believe in reincarnation and karma?"

I suppose so, I can't think of any other belief system that offers better logic. But is it really that simple and obvious?

"Hey sunshine climb into people's heads and find out what's happening. Self-hatred, perverted thoughts, pretense, false emotions, aggression and self disgust. Blind acceptance, ignorance, even self sacrifice, innocence and fear could lead to all sorts of bizarre scenarios. The list goes on. People are generally unaware of what they are thinking and why they are doing things let alone how their other energy centers are responding. For example, have you ever liked someone but felt uncomfortable? Where is this notion coming from? Probably from your base feeling, it's got nothing to do with knowledge in a situation like that. So is it really that simple?"

Okay life and people's thoughts are complicated and perhaps we drag a lot of negative situations into our lives because of our ignorance of ourselves and the world.

"Right. So the next issue. How about precession of the equinoxes?"

Hmm, I seem to remember something. But what has this got to do with our earlier topics?

"It connects believe me."

Okay I think the Greeks first thought of the idea before the birth of Christ. Some thing to do with the fact that the earth's axis describes a cone. Basically it acts like a spinning top.

"Yes indeed, but there are so many variables the math is

complicated as hell."

Ha ha I spot ignorance.

"Hey remember I'm only you and remember one is only viewing space from the vantage point of this planet. So to believe that such changes in perspective of the universe cause anything or affect our lives is but an ignorance."

Great so where are we going with this?

"They are only signs that greater things are happening. Therefore as an analogy: the wheels and cogs and hands of a clock show the time, but they are not the sun in the sky nor the birds singing in the evening."

So?

"So we are entering a new age. It's a clean start for everyone and everything. There is no destiny. We are all free, therefore any intentions and actions return instantly."

Chapter 15

Taiwan

Living and teaching English in Taiwan was a novelty when I arrived, actually to be honest when I really first got here I was shot – that's shot as an adjective – as thought processes jabbered uncontrollably in my mind and I just acted. I suppose I just developed an emergency procedure to survive within my core self by just playing out the sensible moves. Yet I was robotic and vacant and consequently inadequate at the job I had come here for. Originally I had been employed as a children's teacher, their bright faces and innocence had reminded me of my past. Hilda's children had emanated absolute trust and love, which I had eventually ignored and finally rejected. They were no more than an experiment, occasionally meaningful like my garden, yet objects that could be dispensed with when they failed to fit in with the grand scheme I wanted to create. Consequently I failed with my classes as much as I had failed as a true father figure. Sasha and Ivan left with their mother, confused and broken, young adults I would never see again.

Leaving me holed up on the side of a mountain, ultimately ill and living off welfare and finally suffering from schizophrenia, with a terrible feeling of dread building up and the sense that I was rotting away. So one afternoon I had asked for help. I had been humble and desperate. I'm not a religious person, not that I'm against such beliefs, I just feel indifferent. Anyway an answer had arrived a moment later, I was advised to get a job teaching English in Taiwan. Sometimes it was like that, if I became genuinely emotional or upset, an answer would appear reasonably soon or instantly. I couldn't plan on being upset or pretend I was emotionally distraught, and even if I was truly feeling that way and expected or thought I deserved an answer none was forthcoming. Most came when I completely forgot my request. So with this lead I researched for jobs abroad in the local library, all the while the voices continued talking away, making up scenarios that I sometimes got attached to or angry with. These stories would affect me emotionally and I would get carried away with them, it was like a soap opera drama playing in my mind. Eventually I realized they had nothing to do with my reality and I used to crush the narrative by screaming or complaining that it was all make believe. I hypothesized it could be an old part of myself from the past which used to make up things, where I would play out my negative and positive emotions in imaginary situations.

Therefore I developed a habit of asking for such things to be removed so I could concentrate on what I was doing. I researched continually: bookshops, the library, the internet. I applied online numerous times for any jobs in South East Asia. I was determined to leave. Carraigulla now haunted me, everywhere I went I would see my wife's handiwork and hear the children's voices laughing. A mocking in my head. Also the place was not really mine either, I had failed financially as usual, I was about as successful as Vincent Van Gogh. My father had once again come to my aid. I still remember making the phone call begging for help.

I should have never asked or accepted any assistance, I recall his derogatory condescending tone even today. I confess I hid the aid or tried to play it down. Steve the landlord had one day mentioned that he had something important to say, I had driven down to the farm to buy milk as usual and he mumbled that Carraigulla, the cottage and land connected with it would go up for sale, but we would have priority. A feeling of panic had welled up. The old familiar inadequacy, my life a conspiracy to undermine any self-esteem I had painstakingly tried to glean. I gave in again and rang from a call box, with Hilda and the children waiting anxiously in the pub. I had the weird intuition he was expecting the situation, his crisp, scoffing voice spelling out the details.

In the early spring an agency secured me a job in Tainan, Taiwan. I had never heard of the place, but I accepted it immediately, selling all my belongings to pay for the flight, which the company promised to reimburse on my arrival. I landed in the capital Taipei at the end of April. I had fled Carraigulla as everything had slowly died with the break-up with my wife: my new pet dog, my garden, and then eventually my feelings. I had lived alone for two years trying to make a go of it after my summer of madness, yet even though I conquered schizophrenia other 'punishments' rained down on me.

The dog I had bought as a companion became ill one day and subsequently passed away. Hilda had never allowed such pets, stating any animal was a responsibility, a commitment, something I had totally rejected when it came to a third child. I was intermittently ill, money became a problem and Hilda's old friends when I happened to see them appeared to ridicule me. Hilda herself wanted no contact or reconciliation. She had moved miles away to another county to start a new life with her children. So one miserable morning in January I had pleaded for an answer to my misfortune and had been told:
"Any asshole with a degree can get into Taiwan and teach English."

Moving to a city, being immersed in a foreign culture, coping with a tropical climate and trying to teach English took their toll. The weather when I arrived was like walking into my greenhouse on a hot summer's day. I couldn't believe the humidity, I constantly wanted to open an imaginary door and feel fresh air. The traffic stank, the noise grating on my nerves. The people were the only blessing. Most of the time any 'Westerner' will find the Taiwanese very courteous and helpful. For myself in most situations if the language barrier was a problem, somebody would send for help and a person would be found who could speak English adequately, albeit ungrammatically. Verb tenses would generally be dispensed with as the Chinese language may be spoken without them. Nevertheless this situation is pretty wonderful really. My experience in travel is reasonably limited, but the fact remains any Westerner can live and work in the country without any knowledge or reference to the native language of Mandarin. I consider that unusual.

To be honest I found them overly helpful, and I know from personal experience that anyone who is like this may have problems with their personality. Why be subservient? What is there to gain? Was this attitude merely a facade? From my own encounters I would insist most were friendly, curious and delighted to be of assistance. I always found a spark of amusement in their eyes that related to wittiness in their character. Therefore any paranoia on my part might translate this into mocking. But if I opened my heart and feelings rather than perhaps grabbing my anal retentive reserve I always used for strangers, I knew they were genuine considering I was a stranger as well. The whole experience was new and I was forced into confrontations, meetings and dates every day, strangely these encounters were practically a form of therapy, the dehumanization I had gone through as a child was eroded and gradually replaced with a strong sense of confidence.

Unknowingly I was conquering my past, I was finally and truly financially independent: a success. Even the voices matured. Being a 'foreigner' here certainly helped as it attracted attention, but considering martial law ended relatively recently and democracy only began in the last twenty years or so it wasn't surprising. My students seemed oblivious to politics yet I was mistaken; passions and emotions ran high. I was used to Ireland and the UK where the general patter about politics would be found anywhere, like discussions about gardening and the weather. I discovered here most people didn't want to talk about it. Still one day opening the daily newspaper I saw there had been a huge protest about government corruption. The photograph showed protesters had lit thousands of candles which had beautifully illuminated the night. On closer inspection I saw all the candles formed a massive Chinese character. The little caption next to the photo calmly informed the Western readers that the character essentially meant "buttocks or fart".

I was free of my father at last. For the first time in my life *I* was truly autonomous. Carraigulla had been a sham. My own life up until now had been lived in fear. I had been unable to recognize, confront and deal with people properly. The madness was a sort of liberation, ironically pushing me into a full-time job. The company I worked for eventually was a private language center for adults. Initially when I started the premises were rented but eventually they moved to a new building. This whole structure was reinforced concrete built to withstand earthquakes. Yet the design had the sterile feel of the future, even the plants were plastic, the basic accessories steel and glass. But on the top floor I found a bizarre anomaly, in a general area of no specific function stood a garden bench.

An exact replica of a garden bench I had bought for Carraigulla: wrought iron and wood. It triggered my memories, so one afternoon between classes I made my way upstairs and with the place practically empty I decided to doze off, which brought to mind summers where I'd sprawled out in the afternoon in the full sun listening to the usual idyllic cacophony of noises: birds twittering, the hum of insect life, the wind, perhaps the distant chug of a tractor or the lowing of a cow. Only to be rudely awoken by the noise of the traffic from the city below. Therefore my eternal question became how the inside met with the outside? Being content had given me a dream which made me discontent. In achieving independence, becoming financially solvent and building my self-esteem and dignity I had paid a price. I was now living in a city environment I despised. The vision of gentle sunlight and breezes had resolved into florescent lights and the air conditioner blowing into my face. And trying to fathom an answer only produced the conundrum that everything was essentially me. Was this just more mocking? I would admit that sometimes I had bad moods, but more often than not it would be due to my reality. Say for example I would be driving through traffic and some selfish driver would cut me off causing me to break hard and that's when I would lose my temper and curse for five minutes or more. Later I would intellectually consider the possibility that I had indeed been charging something up.

That hatred, that pure rancorous emotion, I'm sure it returns to taunt me. Furthermore why did I meet the careless driver in the first place? Karma? Did I endanger other drivers? I would admit I drove over the speed limit, yet living in the south of the island the road was like a circus, with whole families on scooters, dogs included, bikes on the wrong side of the road and old people in electric buggies wearing milk bottle-bottom lenses. Regardless, I have attempted to be more polite to myself, being aggressive, snide and cynical only drags in negative thought processes. Since the onset of this condition I have tried to find patterns within it, but to no avail. The more sophisticated I have become the more it has, I truly believe I have animated something that is really part of myself. Only occasionally have I received things that I thought were from an external source, but the idea that a creative thought form universe exists haunts me, perhaps literally. All I know is my brain is scrambled and I operate on two different levels, I have my job and my girlfriend yet I am a paranoid schizoid and I cope by chasing and expanding the conversations I have with myself when I am alone.

Chapter 16

There are lies, damn lies and paranoia schizophrenia

Hello everyone in my life. I want to tell the truth. I'm as confused as anyone is as I always see the contradictions in life, the peculiarities and absurdities as you might do. Sunsets, babies' smiles and love are universally accepted as manifold expressions of the Godhead to the wholesome. However my minions report answers to my estranged mind and I know all may not be what it seems. There appears to be no resolute solution to all and everything concerning the masses of humanity, as factions seem to rule our opinions and therefore our lives. Belief systems, conventions, traditions and customs control our minds. Huge thought forms generated by homogeneous milieus invade our brains and manipulate our thoughts. I am no exception yet I like to think I am, even so with my shattered psyche I can pick out the nuances in thought passing through my head.

What is it like to be totally aware of one's surroundings and thinking processes twenty-four hours a day? I wonder? Okay, although I'm a genuine paranoid schizophrenic and I hear voices in my head a lot of the time, over the years I have gotten used to it. After a couple of months of complete insanity, I calmed down and just started talking back and gradually they have become generally reasonable, or so I hope. One of the nastier tricks these thought entities used to play was to inject some emotion into me at times when my 'real' self – "real?" I hear you chortle and snicker – knew it was inappropriate. For example some event would happen in my life and a particular feeling would enter my mind and body, a bit like possession I imagine. Even at the time I would intellectually think and perhaps emotionally react, declaring in my mind and occasionally shouting out loud that it wasn't fair and that I was being manipulated. Later I would complain, yet try to talk in a reasonable way and ask why it was happening. And eventually I started getting various answers such as everybody is surrounded by thought entities, consciousness is connected and thoughts are layered and overlap. A real amusing explanation was: you are not being invaded by anything foreign it is part of your 'old self'. But who was my new self? I had had in the past various clever theories about life, consciousness and the universe, but nothing had prepared me for this.

Basically any of my former suppositions about life were naïve, as when it came to my thought forms they seemed to keep fragmenting and reassembling in some timeless, infinite void. Pure creative thought is limitless apparently. The problem entity that had seized my mind was some strongly enhanced thought form from my childhood that was mainly emotional and very disturbed. A shattered part of my psyche I had developed in this life. The full body was holographic seemingly connecting with everything in the universe on some vague level. It fragmented into major entities that controlled my mind, although really it was me. I persevered and still do in asking questions, shit I had voices in my head, what else was possible? Talk to a doctor? See a psychiatrist? I imagined strait jackets, Phenobarbital injections and a patronizing voice. The entities agreed, but perhaps that was paranoia. Yet my freedom was imperative so I resisted and trying to remain logical I steered a different course.

I have conversations with myself all the time. I am aware that people generally mind chat, that is invent scenarios and stories. Desires and emotions come into play as well and these are enacted in our own mind scapes. Obviously we reflect on and consider the past and present, and also imagine the future. I did it myself before the onset of the madness. Well I theorized that was still happening to me except I was shattered, broken apart. My brain was damaged and these normal conditions had translated into voices. So I decided to take advantage of this speculation. Firstly I attempted to try and temporarily cancel the voices, all the possible scenarios by praying sincerely, not that I'm religious as I've said before. I had been told we inhabit a thought form universe – a fact I still tend to accept – so I imagined a compassionate being that might help me, not that I contacted anyone or anything, but on the whole the scheme worked. Then I started asking questions. Now believe me when I admit I've been influenced before, when the condition first occurred I was unaware and it developed gradually over a number of days and weeks. I was really controlled and possessed by something, my memories of the time are indistinct, weird, detached and my psyche was shattered and paranoid. Enough to say experience acts as a guide and I did not want to become prone or gullible again. My only premise was I was dealing with consciousness and without question I accepted it was limited, due to the fact it was probably my own. I did not want to believe in the idea I could conjure up God the creator of the Universe in my mind or 'Zog' the leader of an alien race, if such beings exist anyway. So introducing various topics I interviewed my 'thoughts'.

Hey how about religion?
"What of it?"
What's your opinion?
"The same as yours."
Hey very funny how about something new.
"Mmm. How about dangerous? Here we are in the 21st century surrounded by technology and pollution, and people still insist on believing in books and writing thousands of years old."
Hey it's called faith and some of it is not that old. Not that I believe in it though.
"The concept is odd though: putting one's life and energy into something that could be complete nonsense. Acting out belief systems that could have no true bearing on what people truly

are and what they could become."

Hey it's a complicated issue. The question of who is right or wrong is unanswerable.

That is why it is called faith.

"Okay here is the truth from *our* point of view. There are only factions. The world is part of a creative thought form universe. 'Good' and 'evil' are part of it. Beliefs, thoughts, intentions and actions belong to their creators. What we create is ours, it is the same for everything."

Okay how about God the creator?

"'God' as a thought form is unknowable for us, the universe is too vast."

Hey people believe in God they pray to him. Not that I think it's male.

"Personal or group deities can be created, it is naturally part of creative thought."

Hey so I could pray to the real creator. I could send my thoughts and prayers to the right one. Ha ha.

"Do so. We will try to take them there personally. Ha ha."

Okay later, let's change the subject. Wait a minute does praying work?

"It does if you deserve it, but that is the wrong word. People attract to themselves what is needed 'good' or 'evil.' "

But how?

"Through their beliefs, thoughts, intentions and actions."

Mmm back to that again, sounds more like a new age hippie universe.

"Ho ho. Hey try this, do something really drastic, 'good' or 'evil' it's up to you and see how what you create stays with you and affects your reality."

It's okay I'll give that idea a miss. I'll keep praying for money, perhaps throw more in the donation box at the seven eleven. Hey how about death, know anything about it?

"Factions again, you go to where you deserve due to..."

Beliefs, thoughts, intentions and actions. Mmm. Yeh I understand.

"You are not truly human in death. You become an entity,

vibrations of everything you were and echoes of everything you might become. An experience that is guaranteed."

Everything I might become?

"Hey don't worry you'll carry this personality. And lots depends on your, yes once again, beliefs, thoughts, intentions and actions. But believe this, death is limited like life."

Mmm how about everything I ever was. What was I?

"All sorts of things."

A monkey?

"Yes I suppose, even interstellar dust and plasma."

I was a rock. Crap. I know what you thought forms are like, taking over my mind and driving me insane.

"Hey believe what you want and create your own faction."

I have anyway and you are part of it.

"Hey look you were a vibration, a signal, part of evolving consciousness, the universe was very young. Matter and thought work hand in hand. Evolution."

Mmm, maybe. So the rocks are evolving now eh?

"Consciousness pervades everything."

Hey how come I evolved to human level and some rocks stayed the same?

"It's a destiny of sorts."

Perhaps it's free will and the rocks didn't want to change.

"Perhaps rock evolution took place in another part of the universe, perhaps intelligent balls of plasma exist elsewhere."

Hey this is going nowhere. Forget it. What about the stuff about the New Age coming. Do you remember? The Albrecht Durer engraving?

"What of it?"

How come the message from the magic square includes such a badass? You know who I mean. Why is it used? Is it a metaphor for something or is it a real person? And why is it appropriate for this so-called New Age?

"The Anti-Christ? More evil in the world than good I suppose. Also Durer was a Christian from the Middle Ages, a spooky and superstitious time to live. Who it may be is up to you. And this New Age is fickle."

Hey that's a bit lame!

"Look, it is a warning that everything is back to zero, so anything one, or I should say anything, does comes back instantly. And if there is more 'evil' in the world than 'good' it's a freaky time."

How come?

"Everything is unstable as there are no strong future echoes ahead, no forthcoming destinies for the world at large and individuals, and more 'evil' influences than 'good.' A potentially negative time."

Okay I'll pray and try to do good deeds.

"Hmm, a good idea I suppose."

Hey just a moment, even though everything is supposed to be equal, some people and things must have a head start, an advantage.

"Granted this may be true, as certain people or things may be physically, mentally, emotionally and spiritually advantaged. Yet all is relative, so being set in one's ways and thinking one is lucky or gifted in a certain way may prove to be false."

I thought belief was important!

"It is, but there are no more absolutes. Everything forges its future instantly. So even though in the past strong beliefs in luck may have turned out to be pivotal. And strongly believing in a faction may have provided great support. They are just fantasies now, as anything you create and do belong to you and affect you directly and immediately."

Surely that is an absolute.

"Do you not borrow from the great pool of thought and perhaps add to it? Every thought, concept and feeling you take and use only connects you to like-minded entities, beings."

The things you mention are like riddles, puzzles.

"Just remember the real terrain of this world is the world of thought, that is the structure that gives the physical world its form. Therefore any outward appearance could well be deceptive."

I didn't want to believe any of it. What started out as a

therapeutic exercise has developed into a surreal philosophical debate and sometimes an argument. I blame myself, I turned it into a game. Granted today's conversation seemed reasonably civil if not outlandish and even 'I' have my mood swings. Also I remember in my youth I had always contemplated and wondered about life, and here were the answers coming back from fuck knows where. My severed mind? I guess the disorder transforms, then again I'm part of it or it really.

I had read about the condition I had developed even with the voices whispering in my head. Hey I know about the fucking delusions of grandeur, the self importance, the secret information, I know about the paranoia. I was beginning to think that I was the motherfucker from Durer's message. To be honest though a part of myself was a smart arse and I reckoned I was talking to it. As a kid with my family, I and my siblings had been constantly groomed for competition and there was this feeling I always had to be right. I'm still like that now as I deal with my class, I want to be in control and never wrong. Furthermore in the past I had always wanted to be special, different, the guy with all the answers, today I suppose I would have been labeled as nerdy.

I had been a bespectacled, hunch-backed, spotty young man who had been bullied by just about everyone and wanted recognition and approval. This may seem like a cliché type of scenario but having a nervous breakdown and developing schizophrenia, then escaping without being detected was I guess unusual. I remember sitting in the doctor's surgery in Ireland as a so-called friend had been 'concerned' and reported me. Shit if he wasn't spot on with his questions, his gaze never leaving me, even towards the end of his little interview his temperament changed and he tried to provoke me. Thank God the bitching voices in my head had the presence of mind to constantly tell me to "lie to the fucker." Something out there or in there valued freedom and self preservation, however these were the same thought entities I now chatted to about esoteric realities or theories, take your pick. Really the amount of bizarre information that has passed through my mind is astounding, as soon as I began this debate idea – a natural response to the surreal condition – the conversations diversified. Some things I believe in myself yet others were and are difficult accept. Nevertheless any rejection of ideas usually later brings in further 'proof' or data into my mind and the voices convince and cajole, trying to push the boundaries of my belief. Therefore when cooking and adding salt to a meal I am reminded that crystals exhibit strange organized patterns, a bit like those first living cells developing from the primeval soup.

These philosophical debates are endless and all I can say is the voices have changed, maybe evolved. It has got to the stage where paranoia schizophrenia is irrelevant, perhaps I can cope. What I want now are genuine answers, yet what I receive is not what I believe or think is credible, and sometimes my conversations degenerate and yield nothing and are meaningless, illogical and even childish. Today's chat as you know insisted that everything is interacting and evolving, challenging any simple view of life, and according to my thoughts I connect with everything and have a karmic relationship with whole of creation. This know-it-all presence reverberates in my head. But this is not always the case unfortunately, as sometimes my thoughts can also be sarcastic, crude, oddball and malicious. Nevertheless please trust me when I say I have tried to cover all the bases and belief has its price. I asked about aliens once and received the comment that soul development in other parts of the universe is a definite: we are them.

Anyway I forgot to mention the quote, the message from Durer: spiraling around the magic square in a clockwise direction, starting at the bottom right hand corner with the number one it reads in Latin: "I Anti-Christ reign from 2005 therefore all that stands between us is love or annihilation."

Chapter 17

Another kind of madness

There is a line of buses but they have no windows and are covered in electric light bulbs, deafening trashy acid house blasts out from concealed speakers. I am dumbfounded. Next, a parade of brightly colored costumed people carrying a large effigy that's wearing Nike trainers passes by. Betel nut juice and spent fire crackers litter the ground. On first sight the vision is fantastic, outlandish, however this is Dao Jiao or Daoism the main religion here. This is their belief, this is their world and they are devout as any other believers in their faith. Ornate temples are found all over the island, deities are everywhere, they create them. To some this festival is an alternative pagan celebration, a massive show of ostentatiousness, yet where does veneration and self love end and degeneracy begin. I cannot judge and choose not to, for me it is a procession, a novelty, a wonder, but no more than an Easter parade, something colorful and exotic, yet still a faction I have no belief in. I have a feeling that the entities that inhabit my mind are right and we are living in a thought form universe, hence there is no real truth, we just invent it, alas we are what we make and are only limited by our imaginations. Science tells us the view of the expanding universe is pale orange.

It is autumn now and my desire to leave this city is growing stronger by the day. However I remain as my funds are low, and I am lazy and complacent. The city stinks yet it is convenient and my Taiwanese girlfriend has other plans. I must admit I am attached to her, the alien manners, broken English and Oriental looks control me. It is ironic though that the very time I believe the world may collapse economically and environmentally I am stuck in a city, for I remember the beautiful havens I lived in. This evening driving to my apartment I recalled being at Carraigulla: sitting in the bath with the dog standing sentinel at the open back door, the night air was blowing in causing the candle I had made from beeswax to flicker. The water was from the mountain spring, the wood that heated it I'd cut myself. I truly felt content.

The city is foul and even though I'm not so idealistic to believe in nostalgia I yearn to return. The entities and their interpretation of Durer's message freak me. I had a conviction the engraving was a warning when I first saw it; the whole composition had a feeling of familiarity. So I take the message I received seriously – a portent – and the trouble it forecasts as something I must evade. Everyday I scan the papers looking for evidence that the world is falling apart, I check news items, current events and opinions that might tally with my vision. And even though it may be folly and impossible to ascertain, I cannot help but try as Durer's omen possesses me. The credit crunch now looms after a short lived energy crisis. There has been a big hullabaloo over the seven-hundred billion bank bailout in the States, two weeks later a freighter at Barranquilla on its way to Mexico was discovered to have two-hundred million dollars worth of cocaine on board. The haul estimated to be just over one percent of Colombia's annual production. Meanwhile Sweden's Johan Eliasch, the CEO of Head, a manufacturer of skiing equipment bought a four-hundred thousand acre – the size of Greater London – area of the Amazon rain forest, commenting that the whole Amazon could be bought and saved for fifty billion dollars. I fail to comprehend the logic of this world, I grasp nothing but nonsense. I really must concentrate more on myself.

So living in a country with mainly Buddhists and Daoists I was influenced to contemplate reincarnation. The voices chatted animatedly about the subject, talking of soul development and I took an earnest interest pondering on who

I might have been in the past. If the theory was true it might offer an insight into my life and destiny. Obviously most people get romantic about the idea and envision famous figures that shaped history. I had fancies of being a legendary influential hero. I wanted to be someone strong and mighty. A protector and fearless warrior, yet enlightened. Spartacus. So one day after work I asked.

So who have I been in the past?

"Various characters."

But who specifically?

"No one special."

Hey I bet you're lying

"Hey look, do you know people often go back to places they inhabited before, the areas they lived in in prior lives."

Really?

"Take you for example. Do you remember Ireland?"

Of course I do.

"Well underneath the house and land at Carraigulla in the strata of the rocks and spread over a reasonably large area are your remains."

From when?

"A long time ago actually. You have had other lives in Ireland. But the remains there are from the Paleolithic age."

Hey wonderful. The Stone Age?

"And you died as a young child."

Okay enough of that. Please tell me something more inspiring, something that relates to my life now.

"Okay right, lie back and shut your eyes. Here it goes."

I hope it's something interesting and relevant.

"Relax."

Chapter 18

A vision of a life gone by

God isn't the ocean blue, Christ I have to laugh at myself. Talk about stating the obvious, but then I'm always like this. "Christ" I say look at the waves, the sunset, the sky, the clouds. Their 'real' realness can be so amazing. The everyday world is a shocking place, yet also a place of wonder and here I am now cutting out a slice of it, my rightful part. I am beginning my apprenticeship thank God. So point of fact is this: my master is teaching me how to observe, measure and evaluate, a requisite for all in our trade. Therefore at all times I must endeavor to concentrate and train my mind to be constantly aware and astute.

Fortunately I'm a natural gaper anyway, or so my mother always said. She always told me I was gifted with a quiet mind, perfect for observation. Right, so here I am with two figures seated in front of me, they don't look happy though, this couple, a man and a woman who refuse to meet my gaze. Her eyes are downcast with long dark lashes brushing her blushing cheeks, his stare is towards the horizon, I can feel his resignation, his sense of hopelessness, I swear he wants to talk but refuses to do so out of stubbornness. Perhaps the likes of me are not worth conversing with, not that I care for that matter, besides I have my work to do and at all times I must remain vigilant.

What we do is develop our gifts, or so my master tells me, and I believe him when he says practice, hard work and God's love will get you where you want to be, but one must be constantly diligent. Even so those other buggers I work with never seem to pull their weight. Never mind, maybe the boss has special plans for me. I hope so. Now these people, the ones in front of me were really special, they were the type that had life where they wanted it... Bugger it, there I go again starting to make things up, losing my direction. I have got to focus like the boss says.

So I must practice, practice, practice. Right here we go once more, the woman has shifted her position, she seems to be looking into the distance with defiance in her eyes now, not that I blame her, 'cause didn't we have our fun. I must admit I didn't partake, I'm not really inclined that way. I could see the boss out of the corner of my eye applauding the proceedings yet watching me at the same time, oh how he likes to keep everyone happy. He seemed perplexed though at my air of fascination and disgust at the event. Shit I'm losing it again rabbiting on. Okay the man has just glanced at me furtively, actually when we left he started a conversation and told me what is going to happen to us all.

Well to be honest it was almost like an angry threat, but who can blame these folks after what they have been through. I'm remaining mum on the whole issue and to be frank again I really haven't a clue. And okay that maybe is a lie. The point is this is my job and yeh I don't like it much sometimes, but that's how we get in favor and promoted. Obedience is important. I was in the boss' study as he calls it and isn't it just splendid with all those beautiful pictures hanging on the walls and fancy ornaments. Anyone can see he has a fine eye. Anyway I was just hanging around, waiting for him to show up and I glanced at this painting. Hey I think it was a portrait, I think that's what you call them, people anyway. And wasn't the man in it just all dressed up and looking rich and wonderful with one of those curly wigs on his head. Just like the geezer here really except his wig is askew now and his clothes are soiled. Never mind he'll have other things to think about soon. The thing is don't we all want those comfy surroundings as we get older, we all want to be people of substance, people who get respect shown to them and to get there we've got to work and make sacrifices. Everybody knows it is an unwritten rule, a law of the universe. So here I am working my shift and doing my best to get ahead. So sorry to the fine lady and gentleman because I am just doing my job. Hey the girl is looking happy and relieved as she's spotted our true direction, the gent seems confused, a little worried and me I'll have to start concentrating on my job more, there's a rip tide going out and I don't want to bugger up.

Great, here we are landing nice and neat on the beach. Boss told me to be quick and not hang around. Just get them out and push back and head for home he said. I feel sorry for them really, so I'll try to be gentle, but I've got to be on my guard as I don't want any trouble. Their hands are bound behind their backs. He's shouting again saying we'll all hang, I'll have to be careful. Jesus they are only being left, it'll be a bit like Adam and Eve. Or something like that. I'm not talking aloud, I'm thinking all this, really I'm too busy keeping an eye on things and I've got my pistol out. All I tell them is to walk up the beach which they do, and then I'm off beating the oars through the surf. God, look at the green water. Boss told me it's the blue sky and the yellow sand mixing in the sea, clever man he is. I've got to watch out for the reef or I'll be joining them, the water's darkening, I'm past the breakers and hitting the swell. I've got my back to the ship and I can see the two figures getting smaller, even so I can make out he's trying to break his bonds and I reckon give him half an hour or so and he'll be free.

Not that it matters as I'll be eating my tea by then and the ship will be out of the bay and heading on a new course. You know even though I'm new here I've been to islands like this before, docked in bays and islets and seen the natives and their fancy ceremonies, dancing away on the beach. God don't those women have firm lithe little bodies. The crew laughs at my staring and fascination, I'll grow up yet my bunk mate says then chortles. But fuck don't I think they have better lives, living on the islands, fruit and veg growing wild in a paradise. I wish I was with the bastards I'd just left behind. Perhaps one day I'll do that, but back to the ship and tea for now. Marvelous there're dolphins playing beyond the reef, I can see their shiny backs in the sun. I'm told people not too far north eat the buggers, what ignorance eh? To eat such friendly God loving creatures. But back to reality, the ship's looming into view and the mates are there with the hoist, even though I can't discern their faces, I can feel their grins.

I'm eating my stew below deck and the sun's just gone down. I bet the two I left are at it, lucky buggers. Funny thing though, just as I saw the dolphins ahead I glanced back at the island, with the thin strip of beach and smudged green mountains and I swear I saw more figures coming out from between the trees. I wonder. Anyway I'm finishing my tea when a mate appears. He reports a good job done and the boss is pleased. I nod and feel proud and keep nodding my head in satisfaction, yet being new here I comment the boss is a clever man leading us all from the East Indies and into the Malay Straits and beyond. It's strange but when one genuinely feels admiration and wants to avoid praise for simple things, one usually attracts the opposite. My mate bows and says truly I'm one of the crew, he really seems to admire *me*. Yet for such a simple task I have my doubts, so I insist it was nothing more than the danger of an ebb tide. He laughs and comments that local politics in this region is like the ebb and flow of the tide, meaning I think we must give and take. We are new here he comments, the boss is making new friends and contacts and likes to present gifts to the local people.

The boss doesn't want to stir up any trouble, after all he has a business to run and needs fresh water and produce and he wants to trade fairly and safely for the good of himself and the crew. I'm a little perplexed but beam in pleasure at being treated with so much dignity. So well done again he comments, his eyes rest on the remains of my tea of pork crackling, he smirks. This bothers me so I insist on finding out the reason for his amusement, the comments on local trade bypassing my mind. He grins and says the locals have their own ways and customs and 'fresh produce' for them is just as important as it is for us. I'm still confused. He coughs and says I delivered their long pig. Well done.

Chapter 19

Consumption

I give up. The vision is vivid and disgusting, I reckon it could be a surreal metaphor of my past and as I am used to such chastening I acquiesce. The voices remind me that through ignorance I have pushed my way selfishly through this life. Once again I have been surprised and chastised I suppose, I submit to the madness as looking for enlightenment is not always a happy pursuit. Accepting oneself, one's desires and the consequences that they may bring is a step towards true awareness. I have the desire to escape the city, the pollution, the stress and noise. I feel trapped in my apartment, the whole metropolis is analogous to a termite colony, the claustrophobia is intense. I remember the beautiful landscapes I inhabited, but shit did I really care. The people from my past barely register in my mind: Jan and Rob, the Granges, all the people I met in Cornwall, my Welsh landlord and Irish friends, my ex-wife and her family and my own. I have little concern, when I mourn, I mourn for the land. I miss the fresh air, the trees, the hills, my garden. These are the things my emotions are attached to. I think I comprehend this vision and whether it is authentic or not it helps me understand myself more and maybe others.

I am mad and yet so is my girlfriend. But I realize that I am whereas she does not. Therefore I know better than to criticize and rebuke her, I can read the pain in her face when we argue. I am not the reason for her distress or anger, I am only a trigger that connects her with her past. Perhaps you misjudge such things or even disbelieve, but I tell you this is Asia and cultural differences apply. A few months ago I took an English conversation class on the topic of foreign brides. The printed literature expounded and exposed the common practice of buying a wife from a poorer nation. I laughed at the idea making jokes about the subject, yet my class did not seem to understand my humor. To them it was a natural occurrence, something that was normal, indeed one or two had real situations in their lives where it had happened: a cousin or a brother had actually traveled to Vietnam, Thailand or Mainland China, perused a catalog, then interviewed and finally chosen a mate. Talking to the class I realized the emphasis was on youth and looks. Hey let's be realistic only a poor family would sell their beautiful daughter. Yet this reality is accepted and sanctified by my students, any witticisms on my part only resulted in the fact that their families were far too rich for such a fate to befall them.

Am I living in a modern society in the twenty-first century? Yes I am and this is part of their belief system, automatically recognized by most and a feature that ultimately turns me on. Alas I cannot escape the delight in my mind when I first discovered this Asian fact of life. I may have in the past feigned disapproval at such things and in my heart I do feel it is unfair, but a base excitement at the idea beat all other feelings. I am but an animal. So when getting a lift from an unmarried associate professor, a man whom I had met through my job, and who is talented, kind and obviously well educated the conversation turned to marriage. He informed me he was off to Mainland China to buy a wife, he said it was time. He was in his early forties like me and now wanted a family. He wanted to buy a virgin perhaps, he wasn't sure. I coughed self consciously, yet...

There is a background hum in my mind, I often pick it up when I'm out and about, you see I'm not really concentrating on anything, I'm just strolling, wandering if you will and the vibration engages itself, constantly thrumming through my head. I was always unaware of it before, but recently it became known to me and I investigated like a true scientist. It seems a breasty, curvaceous thought form throbs in my mind subconsciously alerting me to its reality, an inherent reflex, a bit like the constant few degrees buzz above absolute zero in space after the 'Big Bang', except here the space is between my ears.

My girlfriend was sold as a baby, although this is Taiwan some people were and are poor. For two years she was raised and loved by her adoptive parents who could not conceive a child. She became a princess in their lives, a special gift from the Gods and the State, a surrogate daughter. Fortunately for them and unfortunately for her the woman eventually did become pregnant and 'Anna' was returned to her original parents. Growing up in poverty, ostracized, hated, taunted, and beaten by just about everyone in her true family she ran away at sixteen. The confession from her turned me off and I persevere to control my base instincts. I'm nineteen years older than her: a father figure who fucks her. But unlike her real father I strive to understand her as I'm whittling away at myself, trying to destroy my negative emotions that control my responses. When she is upset which can suddenly occur at anytime or anywhere I can see the madness and pain in her face, thought forms from her childhood possessing her soul.

Chapter 20

Mother of all Mothers: Orchid Island

Her beautiful face twists up into a deformed snarl and I know what's coming next, but I've been through this before and my arms whip up in a smooth, natural reflexive movement forming a defensive 'X' in front of my face – I feel like one of those kung fu actors I've seen in the cheap movies on cable television here. The cup bounces off my left forearm and smashes on the floor. I automatically move forward to apply a restraining hold as the shrieking begins. This is a regular procedure – as I try to maintain a tight grip without inflicting pain I croon soothing placations into her right ear. The sobbing begins and a mocking voice whispers in my head.
"This didn't happen with your wife. Ha ha."
It's true my ex-wife was the best friend I ever had. Memories flood through my mind as Anna's body slackens and becomes a dead weight.

Although Hilda was German she spoke perfect if not accented English. Her pale gray-blue eyes were full of love and care and never strayed from my face in any conversation or exchange. Only towards the end did she turn away, her face filled with sadness. At the onset of our relationship I was but her new babe playing at my life and returning home full of tales of adventure, she was like a substitute mother with a keen pair of ears genuinely ready to listen, understand and appreciate my swagger. Over time with her real children growing up we developed a true friendship, I could trust her completely – her faithfulness and honesty as down-to-earth as the soil in my garden. Whenever a problem ensued or disagreement happened I could count on Hilda's sensitive and forgiving countenance, her strong slim arms reaching out to mine.

I stretch out my hand to Anna and promise that we shall have a holiday. I can see an uncertain acceptance in her young face. The battle has been won again and she flops onto the sofa disregarding the mess on the floor and my continued nodding. Her eyes stare blankly into space as I reach for the dust pan and brush.

We are on the train to Taitung, the electric locomotive having been exchanged for a diesel one and we are now racing through tunnels and over ravines. Anna is in the window seat, her excited face turning to me for reassurance and to point out the landmarks. I smile uncertainly remembering my step daughter's innocence and beauty and the occasional 'family' outings in Ireland.

I recall sitting in a cheap second-hand car I managed to acquire. Hilda sits with me in the front, Sasha and Ivan are in the back. If I look in the rear-view mirror I can see Sasha, she sits neatly with the seatbelt sensibly in position, Hilda grabs my knee and smiles in an intimate and seductive way, I return a blank look and accelerate concentrating on the road. As the minutes go by I glance again at Hilda, her eyes stare ahead, yet I can read in her face a perplexed attitude mixed with her eternal understanding. I know she'll grab my hand when we reach the beach, I know she'll stare into my eyes with concern and devotion. Nevertheless the rear-view mirror calls and I must obey my own instinct, that base feeling that runs my mind.

Anna has fallen asleep her young face resting against my shoulder. We must make our way to Fukang harbor from Taitung, the ferry leaves daily and it's a three hour boat trip. I hope the sea won't be rough. Our destination Orchid Island lies sixty-two kilometers southeast of Taiwan – mostly populated by a Polynesian like culture, the descendants of the Yami Tribe live off fishing and subsistence farming – it remains a backwater, a beautiful haven with hidden 'satanic' secrets.

I watch Hilda and the children make their way cautiously down the worn steps and onto the beach, they are loaded up with paraphernalia: buckets, spades, blankets, folding chairs, bags and lunch boxes. When we arrived I made an excuse of a full bladder and sprinted off without a backward glance, I'm standing on the shoreline now and can see their confused and accusing faces. I try to grin and run forward to help, relieving Sasha of her distressingly heavy load. Hilda looks momentarily irritated but immediately recovers her usual state of mind by dropping all her gear and pronouncing that "here will do." She gives me a covert glance, a bewildered expression on her face due to my mood swings. As I sit on my towel and watch the so-called 'children' run down to the waves laughing in delight Hilda gently massages my shoulders.

I tenderly touch Anna to wake her up, we have arrived at our stop. She pushes my hand away roughly and mumbles something in Chinese that sounds almost like her own real name. I persist in waking her as we must hurry to catch the boat. We make our way along the platform carrying our rucksacks, pushing through throngs of Taiwanese. The ferry sails at three and we have yet to buy the tickets.

With the waves slapping against the side of the jetty and Hilda's calm serene face in my mind, the rhythm evokes the easy love that I found and discarded, the gradual detachment I nurtured and the pounding insanity that took over. I'm roused from the reverie by a jabbing in my back and turning to look I see Anna's cute but scowling face motioning for me to take her bag and climb onto the boat. The voices snicker in my mind. The crossing is choppy with a constant warm breeze blowing over the deck. I look over the rail my clothes flapping, flying fish and dolphins follow in the boat's wake. The vast gray-blue Pacific stretches out towards the horizon, the great mother earth in all her glory crowned by a lapis lazuli dome.

Ivan and Sasha return with buckets full of 'precious stones' and whirled shells, they empty out the 'treasure' for us to admire. Hilda oohs and aahs in genuine excitement and amazement and promises to make necklaces and jewelry from the booty. I hold up the polished glass pebbles worn smooth by the sea, the sunlight shining through them casting the dazzling hues into my eyes.

The low mountains of Orchid Island poke out of the mist as the sun sets. Anna is chatting animatedly in her 'Chinglish'. I love her in such moods, her face is bright with enthusiasm with the boat docking. The island is under-populated with very basic amenities; the Yami live close to nature. A tribal culture that has persevered through much abuse. I stare into Anna's beautiful childlike face as she points out all the sights, nevertheless a vision of my ex-wife's eyes plagues my mind. Sadness and sorrow are reflected there, just like in the troubled waters that surround this island and its nuclear waste facility. Everyone of us makes decisions in our lives and thinks they are for the best. I stick with mine. I feel I made the right choice. As we tread the dim road from the harbor hand in hand I look at the beautiful colorful bands of the sunset and reflect on the ironies of *my* life. But still the voices chuckle and gibber in my head.

"Mammon the monster is alive and well. Don't you see it in the bright lights of the cities? Don't you feel it in the frenzy of shoppers, in the teeming masses that ever consume? The mammon must feed yet its shit is brought here. "

Chapter 21

The final truth

There are many forms of the truth, we each have our own version and sometimes with hindsight and experience that may change as well. I understand now that perhaps I was just as delusional and paranoid before the onset of the schizophrenia. There tends to be a before and after syndrome with a disorder like this, yet I am essentially the same person. And like anyone who is honest with themselves I can look back and see the past for what it truly was. Maybe this condition has even given me an advantage. The garden was indeed an expression of myself, but no more than that, a book, or a painting, an experiment, an idea. A love no doubt, but also an excuse, a distraction, occasionally a lie and sometimes a failure.

The land was certainly bewitching, I'm still haunted by its beauty, but even so this obsession translated into disregard for other matters. The upbringing of the children and their welfare were equal to my care for chickens and ducks, my wife was no more than an old horse put out to grass. I have nothing to say on these issues, I have no long descriptions of events or character assessments, conversations or otherwise. This document is about me and my life, how I acted and how I felt. I am the same as ever, but now I know who I am and so I choose not to get involved anymore. Attaching oneself to people out of habit and insecurity is a stupidity. Whether karma exists or not I look back on the past and know for certain my arrogance, mistakes and fantasies led to others' downfalls and unhappiness. I know now I am not normal, I am certain I have brain damage and the usual emotional responses are lacking. I am a vacuum and was before, perhaps the emotional center of my brain simply does not function properly. I don't know and I will never find out the truth and I don't care. I watch out for myself and my strange new companion. I tend to live in the moment, my mind picking up visual info, sensations and the voices. I keep in touch with my father now, he is over eighty and keen to talk on the phone. I have no hatred or malice for him. What I was told I choose to overlook, maybe it was an accident, perhaps it was congenital. With madness it is hard to trust any feelings.

I have voices in my head frequently. We all have negative thoughts and I am no exception, yet mine possibly chat in my mind and I get the impression I am possessed. I logically think that I am not, but I still must face it everyday. Carraigulla was my playground, a cheap rent and later an acquisition by my father. A man who worked and saved all his life, who was generous enough to invest in a wayward son. That is how I see it now. I'd never had a real full-time permanent job, I scrounged from the welfare, worked illegally and posed as an artist. For thirteen years in Ireland I lived in a make believe land, I was living a delusion long before I ever became mad. Everyone has to face reality, I face it now as I drive through the traffic. I hate it but that is how life is, we hate it and daydream of better things, but whether we get there is another matter. Believe in your faction and love it, and one day you might achieve your desires. I believe in better things for myself.

I have analyzed my mind, dredged and examined my dreams and aspirations, and I know I may have some chance of escaping the drudgery and ugliness I despise. I have looked back to the past and know the transition to madness was a physical step, yet the baggage I carried was the same. So I chose to believe there were no footsteps of the Anti-Christ, no dark curses following me, no secret messages written by a sixteenth century German artist. Only my lonely, sad and deluded ego exists, screaming out for attention in this grim, polluted, overpopulated world.

Epilogue

We consume nature and the rich consume the poor. We all know we feed upon one another. This is the order of life that has been created. Or we have created. Yet as we evolve we may develop compassion. We can pull ourselves up by our bootstraps. A hierarchy of love.